Thoughts of a Grasshopper

Thoughts of a Grasshopper

ESSAYS AND ODDITIES

Louise Plummer

Deseret Book Company
Salt Lake City, Utah

Some of the essays in this volume originally appeared in the following publications:

"Thoughts of a Grasshopper," *Ensign,* August 1988, and *A Heritage of Faith,* Salt Lake City: Deseret Book Company, 1988.

"Audition," *Lake Street Review,* Summer 1984.

"The Madonna Oma," *YM,* December 1986, from *The Romantic Obsessions and Humiliations of Annie Sehlmeier,* New York: Delacorte Press, 1987. Also in *Women of Wisdom and Knowledge,* Deseret Book Company, 1990.

"A Kissy Kissy Christmas," *A Christmas to Remember: A Collection of Favorite Holiday Memories,* Salt Lake City: Deseret Book Company, 1990.

"Wallflower," *New Era,* April 1973.

"Fear, I Embrace You," *Women and the Power Within,* Salt Lake City: Deseret Book Company, 1991.

Library of Congress Cataloging-in-Publication Data

Plummer, Louise.
   Thoughts of a grasshopper : essays and oddities / by Louise
Plummer.
    p. cm.
  ISBN 0-87579-557-9
  I. Title.
  PS3566.L783T46   1992
  814'.54—dc20   91-42637
                                             CIP

Printed in the United States of America

10   9   8   7   6   5   4   3   2

To my parents, Louis and Gay Roos
With love and appreciation

CONTENTS

First Things First

In 1967 in Cambridge, Massachusetts, all our friends were having babies, but we weren't. We had no luck. And so we did what childless couples often do: we went to a pet store and bought a dog for Mother's Day. She was a Yorkshire terrier, six weeks old, as beautiful as any daughter could be, with deep brown eyes that could make you weep. We named her Emily. The cost was an extravagant two hundred fifty dollars, an amount that embarrassed us (we were students at the time), so we told our parents in long distance phone calls that she had been given to us by a vague "someone in the ward." Besides, Tom thought we could make up the money by breeding her and selling each of the offspring for the same two hundred fifty dollars. We could be rich, he said.

When Emily was old enough, we searched the greater Boston area for just the right mate for our daughter and found him in a kennel owned by Mrs. Iris Campbell, a squarely-built woman who bought her clothes from the Land's End catalogue. She reminded me of my mother. Her house was tidy, her living room dominated by an exquisite needlepoint rug festooned with wild roses connected with dark leafy vines. Only one dog was allowed in the house, her pet, a female Yorkie named Fiona, whose hair was fastidiously tied back from her eyes with a red grosgrain ribbon. She let us know what she thought of our intruding by yapping at us continuously from a safe distance. The rest of the dogs were housed outside in kennels kept as clean as Mrs. Campbell's house. It was here that Mrs. Campbell introduced us to Emily's future husband, a small dog, only two and a half pounds, named Winnie. Our dog, we had explained to Mrs. Campbell already, was large for the breed, about eight pounds. She said we should aim for puppies that would grow to be no more than four pounds. "That's the perfect weight for Yorkies," she said. The petite Winnie and our buxom Emily would more than likely produce such a perfect product together. We were pleased and went home to wait.

When it came time for the conjugal visit, we washed and groomed Emily meticulously and tied her hair up in a swatch of narrow multicolored ribbons, which she pawed loose in the car.

Mrs. Campbell let us into her house. Tom held our Emily in his arms proudly.

"She's a good size to have lots of puppies," Mrs. Campbell said, stroking Emily. Her coloring was good too, she said. Tom and I gratefully soaked up these compliments for our daughter.

"Let's see her teeth," she said, spreading the dog's lips apart. "Oh my," she said in an altered voice. "Oh no." She spread the dog's mouth further apart and to the side to have a better look. "You can't breed this dog," she declared. "She has a bad bite!" It was a pronouncement like, "She has leprosy." Yorkies, she explained, should have an overbite, but "this dog," she gestured disgustedly with her hand, "this dog has an underbite." She stepped back from Tom and the dog as if the underbite might be catching. "It's not a trait I can allow to be passed on. As a breeder, I'm responsible for keeping the breed pure. The AKC could take my license if they found out I was breeding my dogs with inferior animals."

Tom's face fell with the phrase "inferior animals," and he held Emily a little closer, a little more protectively, as if he hoped she hadn't heard Mrs. Campbell's criticism of her.

"Where did you get this dog?" she asked.

We told her.

"It's too bad you didn't come to me," she said.

I felt crushed, and it must have shown on my face, because Mrs. Campbell's voice softened. "Of course, if you just want another pet, and if you promise not to sell any pups, then I might . . . "

"Yes," Tom and I said in unison. Suddenly we wanted to be grandparents more than we wanted to be rich. "Yes, that's all we want," I said.

"I really shouldn't . . . ,"she hesitated.

"We promise," we said, eagerly.

And so Emily and Winnie were mated. But in those years, infertility ran in our family, and Emily, as it turned out, was even more barren than I was, because she never had puppies, while I, after a few more years, had four sons.

Some time after the first son was born, I told this story to dinner guests to show how parental we had felt about this dog, who was now no longer our daughter but merely a good pet. I took great pains to describe Tom's crestfallen face. I imitated the way he cradled the dog in his arms when Mrs. Campbell declared her unfit for breeding. I imititated Mrs. Campbell's firm voice when she announced that "this dog has a bad bite!"

From across the table, Tom interrupted my performance: "You weren't there," he said.

"What do you mean?" I asked.

"You weren't there when she announced that Emily had a bad bite. I went out alone with Emily."

"I was too there." I insisted. "I remember everything. I remember Fiona and the grosgrain ribbons and the needlepoint rug—"

"You were there the *first* time we went out," Tom said, "but I went alone with Emily the second time. You weren't there." His lips curled ever so slightly, ever so smugly—an irritating expression in a spouse. "You're deluded," he finished.

Well.

Our dinner guests turned their faces from Tom to me.

"I am not deluded," I said, my voice rising. "I remember the way you looked, the way Emily pawed the ribbons on her head—"

"Emily always pawed her ribbons loose. You've imagined it. You weren't there."

"I was."

"You weren't, and I can prove it."

No one was eating anymore.

"I know I was alone with Emily," Tom continued, "because she sat in the front seat and on the way home, she got so nervous, she threw up. If you'd been there, you'd have been sitting in the front seat, and she would have been in the back. She threw up in the front seat. You weren't there."

This new fact had a vaguely familiar ring about it. Suddenly I felt unsure. "But I remember it so vividly!"

"That, my dear," Tom's voice was kinder, "is because you

live in a fictional world, and in your world, imagination is better than knowledge." Truth spoken by a triumphant husband quoting Einstein. I suppose we finished the dinner, but I never stopped muttering to myself.

That was the first time I became aware that for me the line between reality and fiction is blurred. My fiction is made up of autobiographical details, even though the events of the story are made up. For example, when I wrote my first novel, it took place in the house and neighborhood where I grew up in Salt Lake City, but the actual writing of the novel was done in Saint Paul, Minnesota. When I visited home after completing the novel, I sat on the front porch and had a confused few minutes as I looked up and down the street that I had so carefully described in my novel and wondered if I had invented the street or if it had invented me.

It works the same in reverse. My nonfiction (the *true* stories) are filled with little fictions. The story I told about breeding our dog, Emily, and thinking I was there is absolutely true, but I don't remember the woman's name. It wasn't Iris Campbell, in any case. She did keep a neat house, and she did have a wonderful Yorkshire terrier, a female, but it beats me what its name was. Probably not Fiona. My job is to tell a compelling story and the only way to do it is through "the divine details," as Nabokov phrased it, so that in my fiction, the divine details are often autobiographical, and in my nonfiction the divine details are imagined. And it is all true. That is why in this book essays are intermixed with fiction, with speeches, and with personal letters. It is all the same to me. My hope is that it is one joyful noise for you, the reader.

Thoughts of a Grasshopper

I first became acquainted with the story of the grasshopper and the ant as a young girl—not by reading Aesop's fable, but by seeing a Walt Disney cartoon. In the cartoon the grasshopper fiddles and sings and eats the leaves off trees while the queen of the ants warns him that he'd better prepare for winter too, but the grasshopper continues fiddling and singing. When winter comes, the grasshopper, blue from the cold, can no longer play his fiddle. In desperation, he knocks on the tree where the ants live and begs them to let him in. The queen of the ants gives her "I-told-you-so" speech and ends with, "So take your fiddle and"—there is a long pause—"and play." So the grasshopper earns the warmth and food of the ants by playing his fiddle.

Aesop, in contrast, is not as kind to the grasshopper. When he comes begging for food, the ant merely tells him, "You sang through the summer; now you can dance through the winter."

I remind you of this story so that I can tell you that, even when I was a child, it made me uncomfortable. It still makes me uncomfortable. The story of the grasshopper and the ant makes me uncomfortable because *I am a grasshopper.* I dance in elevators. The second the door closes, I begin tap dancing and flinging my arms wildly about. I make faces and stick my tongue out at the hidden cameras I believe exist in every elevator. When the doors open, I stop short and stare with what I hope is a bored elevator look into the open hallway ahead.

I am a grasshopper. It takes me a full day to dismantle my Christmas tree because I dress up in the decorations. I wrap the gold tinsel around my head like a turban. I make a shawl for my neck from glass beads and paper chains. I have a special pair of vampy red high heels that I wear only on the day I undecorate the tree. Red glass balls hang from my ears. I sing in front of the hall mirror. I sing "New York, New York—if you can make it there, you'll make it anywhere." I don't know who wrote it, but it's the kind of song that can make you a star.

I am a grasshopper. I have never prepared for winter or the Apocalypse. I do have two thousand pounds of wheat that I hope never to eat and a box of chocolate chips that won't last through next week. Last summer I tried to bottle some peaches—the cold pack method—just to see if I could do it. I bottled three jars full. They sit in my freezer like museum pieces.

I am a grasshopper. I live in a metaphorical world. I read and write fiction. I draw pictures. I dance in elevators. I sing dressed in Christmas tree decorations.

But I was raised by ants. My mother and father emigrated

from the Netherlands to America in 1948 with four children. Five more children were born in Salt Lake City. My father was an electrician. My mother kept the house and us immaculately. She knitted us sweaters and baked our bread. Dinner was ready each night at 5:30 on the nose. She taught me the correct principles of work. She forced me to wash woodwork, wax floors, and clean behind the toilet, but my priorities were not the same as hers. My distress is recorded in my journal of 1959 when I was sixteen years old. The first entry reads:

> Mother has just blown her top. I am a lazy bum with no sense of responsibility, and all I do is write stories and draw and visit my friends. According to her I am no good. Which is not altogether true, but not altogether false either. I already knew everything she told me, so she really didn't have to get all fired up.

Another entry:

> I hate to get up in the morning. This morning, Mother started yelling for me to get up at the unearthly hour of 11:00. Then every five minutes, she'd come in and say, "Are you getting up now or not?" Then I would say, "Do I have a choice?" As soon as she leaves the room I lie back down and daydream. I like to stay in bed so that I can daydream.

And finally:

> Mother is mad because she can't find the little top thing

to the pressure cooker and since I was the last one to use
the pressure cooker, I lost it. Well, I didn't.

Even from these excerpts you can tell that I considered
my work to be different from my mother's. I was already writing, drawing, and daydreaming. And I never outgrew it. I
never intended to. If growing up meant leaving behind the
imagination I loved, I didn't want to be grown up, at least,
not in the same way as most of the adults I knew.

As much as I love my mother, I have not grown up in
her image. But I admire her work. I love to open her linen
closet and see the neatly folded sheets and pillow cases, color-
coordinated, meticulously stacked. I like to stand in front of
the year's supply in her dust-free basement and admire the
rows of preserves, of laundry soap, of peanut butter, and of
polyunsaturated oils. I like to see her white — really white —
laundry blowing on the clothesline. I like to ask her for the
kinds of things that I can never find in my own house, like
the negative of a picture taken twenty years ago or a darning
needle. She always knows where such things are.

I clean too. I'm not always on top of it like my mother,
but I do something my mother doesn't do — I write lists of
things I clean up. Here's a list from my journal, dated March
3, 1984, Saturday:

What we found when we cleaned under our bed:

> *Books: one triple combination;* A Mormon Mother,
> *by Annie Tanner;* The Clown, *by Heinrich Böll;* The
> Tin Drum, *by Günter Grass;* An Essay on Criticism,
> *by Graham Hough;* The Labyrinth of Solitude, *by Oc-*
> *tavio Paz; the December '83* National Geographic; *the*

Roseville phone directory; Be My Guest, *by Conrad Hilton; the April '83* Popular Photography; Time *magazine, February 27, 1984; Louise's journal, March, 1977;* The Power of Positive Thinking, *by Norman Vincent Peale; the February '84* Reader's Digest, *including the titles* "My Angry Son" *and* "Advice from Sexually Happy Wives"

One set of Tom's office keys

A photograph of Sam and Louise

A photograph of Tom and completed jigsaw puzzle

A letter from Roseville schools about Jonathan's registration

Dishes: one red mixing bowl; two saucers; two mugs; one kitchen knife; one empty cherry-cola can; one empty Häagen-Dazs chocolate-chip carton with lid; one Melmac cup

One Rotex labeler

One broken toothbrush holder

One photograph of Dave and Sue Salmon and girls

One empty raisin carton

Four black lead pencils

One red lead pencil

Five felt-tip pens

One ballpoint pen

One roll of packing tape

One cloth handkerchief

One pair of pantyhose

One black high-heeled shoe

One plastic race car

One page from the church directory

Two pen caps

One broken dart
One hanger
One bank-deposit slip
One seminary worksheet (Exodus 24, 25, and 27)
One white shoelace
One yellow wrapping ribbon
One Roseville bank envelope
One disposable razor
Three yellow legal pads, one filled with notes on how
to get rich, including the title "You Can Negotiate Any-
thing"
One stake directory
One plastic action figure
One pair of scissors
One metal whistle
One roll of toilet paper
Notes by Tom on developing a seasonal recreational
facility for ultralite planes, golf, fishing, horseback riding,
cross-country skiing, and key words from Norman Vincent
Peale: visualize, prayerize, actualize.
One empty Kleenex box
One score sheet from Yahtzee
One belt
One piece of chalk
One orange peel AND
One popsicle stick

I'm not completely comfortable with this list, just as I
haven't always been comfortable with being a grasshopper. I
always wondered if there was room in a family of ants for a

grasshopper, room in a community of ants for a grasshopper, or room in a church of ants for a grasshopper. My discomfort, I believe, comes from my fear of disapproval, my fear that ants will not accept me unless I am just like them.

I take comfort in Flannery O'Connor's short story, "Revelation," in which Mrs. Turpin, a middle-aged Christian Southern woman, views mankind as a hierarchy: "On the bottom of the heap were most colored people; . . . then next to them — not above, just away from — were the white trash; then above them were the home-owners, and above them the home-and-land owners, to which she and Claud belonged. Above she and Claud were people with a lot of money and much bigger houses and much more land" (*Everything That Rises Must Converge* [New York: Farrar, Straus and Giroux, 1978], 195).

At the end of the story, Mrs. Turpin receives a vision that destroys her delusion of a hierarchy. She sees a "vast swinging bridge extending upward from the earth through a field of living fire. Upon it a vast horde of souls were rumbling toward heaven. There were whole companies of white trash, clean for the first time in their lives, and bands of black niggers in white robes, and battalions of freaks and lunatics shouting and clapping and leaping like frogs. And bringing up the end of the procession was a tribe of people . . . marching behind the others with great dignity, accountable as they had always been for good order and common sense and respectable behavior. They alone were on key. Yet she could see by their shocked and altered faces that even their virtues were being burned away" (ibid., 217–18).

I like this story because it is about redemption. Without

the atonement of Jesus Christ, our virtues, whatever they are, are meaningless. We are all equally human.

King Benjamin asks, "Are we not all beggars?" (Mosiah 4:19).

"What about works?" someone may ask. "Don't ants work harder than grasshoppers?"

No. Grasshoppers work *differently* from ants.

I would like to rewrite the ending of "The Grasshopper and the Ants" like this: It is winter, and the grasshopper is walking in the snow, talking to herself and answering herself. She wears a yellow slicker over her sweater, because she can't find her parka (which is buried in the debris under her bed). Because she was out of groceries this morning, she is eating a brownie with a carton of milk bought at the 7–Eleven which, thank heaven, is open 365 days a year. The door in the tree where the ants live swings open. The queen ant appears and says to the grasshopper, "We are bored to death. Won't you tell us a story or at least a good joke? Our teenagers are driving us crazy; maybe you could write them a play to perform, or just a roadshow? Do you have any ideas for a daddy-daughter party?"

The grasshopper replies that she has ideas for all of them. So the ant invites her in and seats her at a spotless kitchen table with pencil and paper, and the grasshopper writes the roadshow.

The ant feeds her guest a slice of homemade bread, fresh from the oven, and a glass of freshly squeezed orange juice. "How do you get all of these ideas?" she asks the grasshopper.

"They come to me," says the grasshopper, "while I am taking long hot baths."

I am a grasshopper. I work hard at writing, at teaching, at singing and dancing, at mothering. I have taught my four boys some grasshopper ways. They all can make chocolate-chip cookies and brownies without a recipe.

My mother used to say, "I don't know where you came from." This bothered me, because if she didn't know, I certainly didn't. But I found out where I came from years later when I went back to Holland for the first time since I was five years old. I stayed with my paternal grandmother—Oma—who lived in Utrecht. She set her alarm for nine o'clock in the morning. When I saw that, I knew where I came from. I came from Oma.

I came from you, too, Mother. Otherwise, I would never clean under my bed.

I came from God.

Easter Talk

I remember as a teenager of about nineteen having a discussion about death with my parents at the dinner table in our kitchen. It is my father's voice that I recall most distinctly. He said, "The older I get, the less worried I am about dying." And then he turned his head to my mother and said, "Don't you find that's true?" She didn't speak but nodded in agreement. My father was about forty-five years old at the time. I was comforted to hear that as I got older I would naturally grow accustomed to the idea of my own death.

Now I am forty-five years old and am very much my father's daughter, and I know that he did not quite speak the truth, although he may have thought so himself at the time. I believe he felt safe after a meal of beef and red cabbage spiced with caraway seeds the way only my mother can make it. I believe he wanted to take care of me — to quell my anxiety about death. I believe he saw a teaching moment and wanted to teach. Since then his blood pressure has risen, along with his cholesterol. He has experienced hours of heart palpitations. Since then he has had prostate surgery. I have seen the terror

in his eyes. My father doesn't want to die any more than I
do.

I look through the family photograph album and see myself
at six months old, lying on my stomach, fat and healthy. I
turn the page and I am six years old, blonde hair trimmed
close to the ears in a Dutch cut. Then I am thirteen, playing
the flute in front of the Christmas tree. I am seventeen wearing
a straw hat with a wide brim posing with a paint brush behind
an easel like Van Gogh. I flip the pages through wedding pictures, through babies, who are now themselves teenagers. And
I see it clearly. I have been dying from the beginning.

I see women five years older, ten, twenty, forty years older
than I am. I see their puffy eyes and creping necks. I see the
canes and the crutches. I see their bodies maimed by surgery,
by paralysis. In their faces, I see my future. I am dying.

I don't want to die. I have enough energy, enough ideas,
enough talent, enough passion to live a thousand years. I want
to continue writing, teaching, singing Beatles songs with
Charles in the car speeding along I-15; I want to continue
crooning "Mr. Sandman" with my four sisters the way we have
done since we were young. I want to sit on the front steps of
my house and watch the changing light on the mountains at
twilight; I want to have lunch with Elizabeth; I want to play
backgammon with Tom and drink hot chocolate from my best
china cups. I want to continue taking steaming, hot baths. I
want to learn to tap-dance and speak French. I want to speed
in an open convertible from here to Mirror Lake and back.

I want to live forever.

There have been times in my life when I have been tempted
to succumb to the despair that afflicts so many twentieth-century

minds. Vladimir Nabokov summarizes it: "The cradle rocks above an abyss, and common sense tells us that our existence is but a brief crack of light between two eternities of darkness" (*Speak, Memory*, rev. ed. [New York: Perigee, 1966], 19).

But everything I am, my whole being, shrinks from Nabokov's notion of eternal death. I have been healed and comforted by priesthood blessings. I have realized the promises from my patriarchal blessing. I have felt the whisperings of the Spirit, and it tells me that I have lived before, as it says in the Doctrine and Covenants that "man was also in the beginning with God" (93:29). It tells me I am God's child.

All my life I have been surrounded with good people — including my parents. If I have sensed my father's fear of dying, I have also sensed his faith that calms that fear. If I have seen women, older than I am, aging ahead of me, growing sick ahead of me, dying ahead of me, I have also seen their courage, their buoyancy, their righteousness, their faith that life extends beyond this life. I have seen the light of Christ shining out of their faces. Their goodness and kindness buoys me up. Their faith reinforces my own. I have felt a part of the community of Christ — in this ward and in other wards. I love and need to be part of that community.

I choose to listen to the voice of Christ. It is a compelling voice: "I am the resurrection, and the life: he that believeth in me, though he were dead, yet shall he live: and whosoever liveth and believeth in me shall never die" (John 11:25–26).

I choose to replace the unbelieving voice of Nabokov with the vision of Thomas Wolfe: "Something has spoken to me in the night, burning the tapers of the waning year; something has spoken in the night, and told me I shall die, I know not

where. Saying: 'To lose the earth you know, for greater knowing; to lose the life you have, for greater life; to leave the
friends you loved, for greater loving; to find a land more kind
than home, more large than earth—Whereon the pillars of
this earth are founded, toward which the conscience of the
world is tending—a wind is rising, and the rivers flow' "(*You
Can't Go Home Again* [New York: Harper and Row, 1981],
576).

Audition

When I learned in 1975 that the Minneapolis Stake was sponsoring a performance of the Book of Mormon Oratorio, I wanted to sing in the chorus. The performance was a joint effort between the University of Minnesota Symphonic Chorus, conducted by Dr. Dwayne Jorgenson, and the Civic Orchestra of Minneapolis, conducted by Dr. Clyn D. Barrus, who was also a member of the Saint Paul First Ward. I asked Clyn if I could participate, and he told me to attend the Symphonic Chorus rehearsals and to tell Dwayne Jorgenson I was there, which is what I did. But after two weeks of rehearsal, Dwayne began urging me to audition, as the other members of the chorus had to do. I told him I wasn't really signed up for credit in the class and would prefer not to. He said he'd like me to audition. I said I'd rather have polio. Finally, after much good-natured bullying on both sides, I decided to write my audition. This is it:

Professor Dwayne Jorgenson, Conductor
Symphonic Chorus
University of Minnesota
Minneapolis, MN 55455
November 15, 1975

Dear Professor Jorgenson,

I agree with what you said during Symphonic Chorus prac-
tice this evening: no one is officially enrolled in Music 1001
until she has had an audition with you. Let me say that I think
that is fair. Very fair. I agree with you one hundred percent,
sir. The problem is that I am not enrolled, nor do I want to
be. I just want to sing in this one concert. An even bigger
problem is shyness. I am an extremely shy person and am, for
that reason, particularly pained with the idea of Singing All
By Myself For You. That is, I don't have a "solo" personality,
if you know what I mean. Still, I want more than anything
to sing in your chorus, because your good works are known
throughout the entire Minneapolis–St. Paul area. But I am
shy about the audition. It just kills me to think about it.
However, I have come up with a solution which, I think, will
satisfy us both.

I will write my audition for you. You can read it and make
a judgment. This method does have some disadvantages: it is
difficult to hear the quality and tone of the voice in a letter.
I will be honest. My voice is a cross between Carol Burnett
and Wayne Newton with a heavy nasal twang that remains
even when I cover my teeth with my upper lip as you so
adequately demonstrated for us today. The other disadvantage
in writing my audition is that I am, by definition, the author
of my own audition. Trust me. My best friend, Mary Beth
Kellendonk, has auditioned with you and has told me in detail
what is required.

PAST CHORAL EXPERIENCE: I sang third alto in the
Alexander Pope Municipal High School A-Cappella directed
by Ms. Francine Crow, a former pupil of yours, who quoted

you as saying that music was the window of the soul. We sang
"Master of Human Destiny," "Oh Brother Man," "Waters
Ripple and Flow," and "I Left My Heart in San Francisco."

I also sang in the chorus of the Falcon Heights amateur
Opera Association's Summer Festival production of *Tannhäu-
ser.* It was directed by Heinz Schlenker, who was born twenty-
seven miles from Wagner's birthplace and who immigrated to
America at age three months. I was a pilgrim and a lady in
Hermann's court (Hail, Hermann, Hail).

I am presently the only tenor in our church choir.

OTHER MUSICAL EXPERIENCE: I play the ukelele.

VOICE RANGE: First, I shall sing in my lower range
beginning at middle C and ending with low B, beyond which
I just grunt. Here goes:

La La La La La La La La La

Now for my upper range — beginning at middle C and
moving up:

La La

As you can see, I have the range of Nancy Sinatra. Actually, when I am in good voice I can go up comfortably another
octave. Due to a chronic nose and throat problem — I have a
deviated septum — I have not been in good voice since 1967.

SIGHT READING: I shall read from an aria in *Israel in
Egypt* by George Frideric Handel. I have a whole book of arias
that I bought in a moment of disgusting confidence. I assure
you that I am sight reading. I have not had many opportunities
to sing arias. I hope you realize that I am very nervous about
this part of the audition. I can hardly breathe and my palms
are perspiring. In fact, I'm sweating like a hog. You may want
to read this aloud so you can hear me better. I shall begin:

How was that? I hope you will not hold it against me for having a quivering voice on account of the shyness. The quiver goes away when I sing in a group. Anyway, I feel better now that this part of the audition is over.

RHYTHM: I shall now clap out the rhythm of the first line of the aria for you:

Clap Clap Clap Clap Clap Clap Clap Clap Clap Clap

SOLO SELECTION: Mary Beth said that you also required a prepared piece, so I have practiced an aria from J.S. Bach's *Christmas Oratorio*. I will try to sing a little louder this time, and I will accompany myself on the ukelele.

> *Prepare thyself Zion, with tender affection,*
> *the purest, the fairest, this day to receive,*
> *the purest, the fairest, prepare thyself Zion,*
> *with tender affection. Prepare thyself Zion*
> *with tender affection, the purest, the fairest,*
> *this day to receive, prepare thyself, Zion,*
> *with tender affections —*

That was lovely even if I do say so myself. I'm sorry about the ukelele string breaking in the middle of it.

Thank you for reading my audition. Please let me know if I made it, and don't forget to fill out an audition slip.

Sincerely yours,

Louise Plummer

This audition did its magic. After Dwayne Jorgenson read it, he said, "You can be in my choir anytime." He never did hear me sing.

The Madonna Oma

In some other world, not the one I lived in, beautiful people gathered in the evening, sat on their satin-covered bottoms at a table decked out in Lenox china, and ate a civilized meal of exotic dishes like breast of unicorn. Their eyes feasted on unpronounceable flowers — anemones and forsythia — bunched artfully in silver urns. I knew it existed. I saw it in a glossy magazine, and I wanted a perfect life like that. Photographs don't lie. Do they?

We ate in the kitchen on a table spread with a vinyl cloth that Henny and I wiped down with a damp sponge after the dishes were cleared. Our eyes feasted on linoleum. Yet our kitchen had a glittering cleanness about it that I appreciated, and Mother hid the dirty pots and pans in the oven while we ate dinner. That *was* civilized. It was the dinner conversation, or rather the lack of it — the spats — that depressed me, and they were Oma's fault. She was the cause of our mealtime fights. Like the dinner when Jack Wakefield called me on the telephone for the very first time.

Oma was refusing to eat, her lips held shut in a stubborn, tight line, and Mother simply wouldn't let it be. She was afraid

Oma might starve herself. Fat chance. Oma ate Oreos on the sly.

"Please have some soup now," my mother pleaded, soup spoon poised in the air in front of Oma's clamped lips.

Oma, her arms folded across her chest, turned her head away from Mother. Her hair fell loose from the knot in back of her head. She looked unkempt, like pictures of old people in rest homes I had seen. Sometimes I thought she smelled different too — not a good smell, either.

"Open wide," Mother said. You'd have thought she was talking to a one-year-old.

Oma shut her eyes, wrinkled her nose, and did not open her mouth wide.

"Eat your dinner now, Riet," Father said, buttering a roll. "She'll eat when she wants to."

"She never eats," my mother said.

"She eats all day," said Henny. "She's in the refrigerator whenever she thinks no one's looking. She ate all the Twinkies last week."

"She's not going to get better if she doesn't eat properly," Mother insisted, implying that Twinkies kept one senile and the minute Oma changed her diet she would be herself again. I couldn't believe it.

"Eating is not going to make her better," Henny said. "Nothing is."

Mother offered Oma a buttered roll.

"I hate it," said Oma in Dutch, through her teeth.

"Then *I'll* eat it," said Henny, snatching the roll from Mother's hand. "I love them."

As soon as Henny bit into the roll, Oma wanted it back.

If she was not interested in eating, she was interested in possession, and it was *her* roll.

"Give it back," she shouted. "It's mine."

That was when the telephone rang.

"Give it to me," Oma cried.

I got up and answered the phone, which sat on a small table in the hall adjacent to the kitchen.

"You don't want it, so I'm going to eat it," said Henny.

"Hello," I said into the receiver.

"Tell her to give it back!" Oma yelled. She began wailing.

"Hi, this is Jack."

"Jack." Unbelievable. Old Spice aftershave seemed to waft through the telephone receiver. Jack Wakefield was calling me.

"Henny, stop teasing your grandmother," Mother said.

"Can we eat in peace, for once?" Father asked Henny.

"How are you?" asked Jack.

Not fine. Not fine at all. And marvelous. Never felt better. All of the above.

"Fine," I said. The kitchen was exploding with noise.

"What's going on?" he continued. He could hear everything, I was sure of it.

"Oh nothing," my voice was serenely casual. "My grandmother sometimes gets upset at dinner." I put one finger in my free ear.

"Your grandmother?" he asked. I could hardly hear his voice.

"People who don't eat don't get anything," Henny taunted Oma. She picked up the entire basket of rolls and held them above her head.

Oma, frantic, howled like an animal.

"Henny!" My father's balled-up fist smashed the table surface. Dishes clattered.

"Are you eating dinner?" Jack asked.

"No. I mean, yes. Can I call you back in a few minutes?" I couldn't believe I was making this request, but Oma was bawling so loudly I couldn't concentrate on his voice. I didn't want him to hear her. I didn't want him to hear my whole crazy family.

"Okay, I'll talk to you in a few minutes then. Bye." I was sure he had heard everything. Good-bye, my love. Jack Wakefield had called me, and I couldn't talk to him.

"Why should the rest of us have to listen to her whining all through dinner?" Henny shouted at Father.

"You make it worse when you tease her." Father's hands were still fists. It occurred to me that he wanted to punch Henny, and even though I was mad at her too, the thought made me sad. We were so far from those Lenox china advertisements.

"I can't stand it," Henny screeched. "Every night Mother begs her to eat. Just let her alone!" She had turned to Mother.

Oma had parts of three rolls stuffed into her mouth, chewing on the dry bread and watching Henny to make sure she wouldn't get them back. Fat crumbs fell from her mouth onto the table.

"See, *now* she's eating. Are you satisfied?" Henny pushed her chair back and stood up. "You don't have to beg her." She sneered at Mother. "You just have to steal it from her."

"Henny, sit down!" Father's face was white.

"I will not sit down. I hate this family. Hate it, hate it."

She knocked her glass of milk over, swerved around to the back door, and was gone. The walls shook with the door's bang.

For a second we all watched the milk spread across the vinyl cloth and drip into Oma's lap. Oma began crying all over again. The rest of the bread fell from her mouth.

"I'd like to kill her," Father said. I believed it.

"Let her be," Mother said. Her head nested in her hand. "It's not her fault." She shaded her eyes with her fingers.

"Then tell me whose fault is it?" exclaimed my father. No one answered. I had never seen him so mad. This was dangerous. I felt it.

It is Oma's fault, I thought. I wiped the table and Oma with a dishtowel and told her to hush. She continued weeping noisily. I wish you would die now. A part of me—the good part—was shocked and sorry I had thought such a thing; but another part agreed that it was Oma, as she was now, who was the center of these all too frequent fights.

I tried hard to remember the Oma of before, her hair thick, humming morning hums that nurtured a small girl. Oma, picking asters out of her garden on Poorstraat and arranging them perfectly in a blue Delft vase. Oma, my link to the civilized world of the glossy magazines. There was a light about her then, like Madonna paintings; or was that my imagination? This woman, this present Oma, weeping and choking on bread, her nose running—she wasn't the same person even. There was no resemblance between the two. This person was the one I wanted to die. Not really, of course. Not really. I hope I didn't mean it. Mother's head was bent over the table. I didn't mean it, Mother. Erase. Erase.

Erase it with Jack Wakefield. I pictured Jack's family dining in formal clothing, drinking wine from Waterford crystal. I returned to my place and ate my soup in silence.

After dinner, I sat with Oma out on the front porch while Father and Mother attended English lessons at the junior high across the street. Henny had not returned. I was sure she was hiding out at Farrah's until she cooled off. Henny almost lived over there lately. I had tried to call Jack once, but the line was busy. Now I was stuck with Oma. We couldn't leave her alone. She either grew frightened like a child, calling loudly for my mother, or she wandered off down the block, forgetting the way home. Often she sat on Mr. Eberley's porch, repeating my grandfather's name. Once Mrs. Spivack, our neighbor, had called to say that Oma had walked into her house and was napping on her bed.

We sat in the green, painted metal chairs behind the porch railing and the climbing roses. The neighborhood smelled clean, green. *The Thorn Birds,* the book Maggie had lent me, rested in my lap. I hoped to read it while we sat. Already I wanted the handsome priest, Ralph de Bricassart, and the young Meggie Cleary to become one flesh, as it said in the Bible. At least I thought that's what it said in the Bible. Colleen McCullough was not going to gratify me too quickly on this score. Oma was humming softly. I picked up the book. She stopped humming.

"Do you remember me — what I was like — before the car accident?" I was startled by this completely lucid question from her. She was so crazy most of the time. I lay the book down again.

"I used to read a lot too," she mused.

"I remember," I said. It was only a vague memory.

"You are a lot like me," she continued. I wanted to disagree and perhaps she saw this expression, because she added, "The way I used to be. You are like I used to be." I thought again of the asters in the Delft vase, but I couldn't think of anything to say. She wanted a response from me, but I couldn't make one.

"You even look like me." She stroked my cheek briefly and then looked out to the street. A blue Ford truck burning a lot of oil sputtered its way up the steep hill.

"I was young once," she repeated. "Like you."

"Annie, hi!" Jack Wakefield's red scooter jerked to a stop at the curb in front of our house. He wore white shorts and a T-shirt and held a tennis racket. He parked the scooter and walked to the porch.

Oma's face hardened immediately at the sound of his voice.

"Jack!" My voice didn't sound like my own. "I tried to call you, but the line was busy." I pulled my feet down from the porch railing and tucked my skirt modestly under my legs.

"I know. My brother Milton was on the phone. I decided to stop by on the way to the courts." He glanced at Oma. "I'm Jack Wakefield." He extended his hand for Oma to shake. Oma sat tight-lipped and stared straight ahead.

"She's senile," I whispered. "And she doesn't understand English." I didn't want him talking to her. I just never knew how she would react. It was bad enough having her sit there like a stone. My face felt about two hundred degrees, and I was sure my neck was developing those ugly red splotches. Soon he would know that I was a person susceptible to rashes. Unclean.

"Oh, I'm sorry," Jack whispered back. He smiled at Oma and nodded to her. He was irritatingly polite.

"You're going to play tennis," I said, trying to veer his attention away from Oma.

"Yes, I'm meeting Tom Woolley." That was the first time I heard Tom Woolley's name. Jack's tall frame leaned against the porch. "I was wondering if you'd like to . . . "

"*Geef hem niets te eten ook al bedeld hÿ er voor!*" interrupted my grandmother. I felt my neck definitely redden. No question about it.

"What did she say?" Jack asked.

"She said not to give you anything to eat, even if you beg for it," I said. I would have made something else up if I could have thought of anything.

"Tell her I just stopped by to say hello," he said.

"Let's just ignore her," I said quickly. "She'll stop if we ignore her."

"Annie, she's your grandmother." Jack had a wretched respect for the elderly. "Tell her," he insisted. He made a gesture with his hand that indicated I should get on with it.

I told Oma that Jack had come by to visit us both and that he didn't want anything to eat. Jack seemed pleased to hear me speak Dutch.

Oma jumped to her feet with surprising vitality and waved her fist fiercely at Jack, who drew back involuntarily. "Liar," she yelled at him in Dutch. "You've come to steal the potatoes and leave us here to starve. Get out. Get out of here." She leaped forward to the stairs. Jack backed down the front walk. Oma grasped the garden hose, turned the spigot, and aimed the spray directly at him, catching him full in the face. Jack

dropped his racket and spluttered, "But I'm not even hungry."
He started the scooter and sped awkwardly away.

"She thought you were stealing potatoes," I called out
after him, but he was gone.

"You stupid woman!" I turned on Oma. "You stupid, stupid
woman." I yanked the hose from her hands and wrapped it
imperfectly around the spout next to the porch. "How could
you do such a thing?" I yelled. Her disheveled head was bowed,
her shoulders sagged. She reminded me of an abused dog. I
wanted to hit her.

"Go into the house," I said, picking up Jack's tennis racket
off the lawn. I wiped it with my skirt.

Oma stood inside the screen door looking out at me. "He'll
come back to get it," she said plainly and disappeared into
the house.

I hoped it was true.

Across the street, on the playing field next to the school,
a man in white pants and shirt guided a model airplane by
remote control. It buzzed in the air like a tin insect. I wanted
to fly too — spell Jack's name with my white breath across the
sky. I wanted to be transformed into some magnificent glittering creature in a silver, sequined gown by Bob Mackie, who
designs dresses for movie stars, and gauzy wings designed by
God, and hover over the neighborhood while ordinary mortals
like Farrah Spivack stared at me in awe, calling my name,
pleading for my autograph from the sidewalk below.

I walked into the house. Oma sat asleep in the recliner,
her jaw hanging slack, arms folded across her stomach. The
skin on her hands was loose and translucent, the blue veins
bulging in a way that made me shrink back. My own hands

were smooth as porcelain, the veins only pale blue lines map-
ping the surface. Then I noticed it. The veins in my hands
were the same configuration as Oma's. Exactly. I held my
hand, fingers spread, close to hers. Exactly the same. "You
are a lot like me." Oma's words boomed in my head. "The
way I used to be." I fought the idea that her hands were ever
as smooth as mine. I fought the possibility that someday I
might be old and forgetful and that someone young and smooth
and pretty as Meryl Streep would yell at me and call me
"stupid."

Quietly, so as not to awaken her, I covered her with a
knitted afghan. I covered the hands that were like mine and
remembered the other Oma, the Madonna Oma, holding me
on her lap. I leaned forward and kissed her face. "I still love
you, Oma," I said.

Talk for Jonathan's Missionary Farewell

I don't shop at the K-Mart in Orem anymore. I used to go there when we first moved from Minnesota and rented a house in Orem. In those days, I frequently stood in one of those interminably slow checkout lines to become the unwilling witness to someone abusing her child. These scenes usually went something like this: A mother sets down a child, no older than two years, in an aisle and commands in a voice loud enough for all nearby K-Mart shoppers to hear: "*Now, I'll put you down, but you mustn't touch anything. Do you hear me? YOU MUSTN'T TOUCH ANYTHING. If you touch anything, I'll slap you. Do you hear me? No touching.*"

Then the mother moves her cart up the aisle, either talking to a friend or interacting with an older child. She expects the two-year-old to follow her. But the child does what all two-year-olds do: he touches things. He pulls things off the shelf. He removes lids and boxes. He drops those desirable things onto the linoleum floor. His mother hears him drop them, and she turns and sweeps down on him in a rage.

"I told you not to touch anything," she yells and cuffs him soundly around the head. The child cries now, because he's been hurt.

"Don't cry, or I'll slap you again." The mother spits her words out. "I said, don't!" He cannot stop crying, of course, because of her threat, so she swats him again.

My sympathy is more with the child in these scenes. I sense his humiliation at being treated so unfairly. I also feel the mother's frustration and recognize perhaps a dark corner of myself.

Years ago, in Cambridge, Massachusetts, in summer, Jonathan was less than one, and I was very pregnant with Ed. I liked to walk him, then, in the stroller into Harvard Square, a mile from our apartment. We walked either down Mount Auburn Street, where we could see the sailboats on the Charles River and the Boston skyline in the distance, or down Brattle Street, past Al Capp's house, past Longfellow's house and the Cambridge Ward Chapel. Jonathan drank juice from a bottle. He sat in a harness, because if the truth be known, he *despised* riding in the stroller. Yet I insisted on this ritual a couple of times a week, thinking he would eventually adjust. He never did. When we got to the shops, he would try to stand in the stroller despite the harness. I would bribe him with candy or more juice. I would say, "Just a few more minutes."

Eventually he would scream and arch his back and rage at me with his baby fists, and I would try to squash him back down into the stroller. I couldn't let him out, because he couldn't walk. I couldn't carry him, because he was too heavy, I was too pregnant, and the way was too far.

Once, on the way home, when he stood, delicately balanced inside the harness, screaming until his face shone crimson, and I stood with swollen ankles and body, exasperated to have to bend and pick up a plastic bottle he had thrown onto someone's lawn, a nicely dressed middle-aged woman walked by us on the sidewalk. She stopped briefly and in a sympathetic voice, said, "Oh poor baby."

Like a savage, I sputtered at her: "Poor baby?" I said, "What about me?"

She looked at me then the same way I look at those K-mart mothers — with horror. "I'm sorry," she whispered, and hurried away.

I was so deeply ashamed that I have never forgotten the incident even though it happened more than eighteen years ago. My frailty is like that of the mothers at K-Mart, and I don't go there anymore, because I don't want to be reminded.

Recently I reread Aranka Siegal's book *Upon the Head of the Goat,* a story about a Jewish family in Hungary at the time of the Nazi invasion. Mrs. Davidowitz, the mother in the family, argues with her friend, Mrs. Gerber, about the difference between the theater and ordinary life: "Yes, Charlotte," she says to her friend. "If we were given a preview of life's moments of crisis, a chance to think instead of having to act in haste, we would not have to go through life blaming ourselves for not having acted properly. That is the big difference between life and the theater. Rehearsals" (New York: Farrar, Straus, Giroux, 1981, p. 174).

I could have used some rehearsals with Jonathan. Now I wonder why, instead of trying to change Jonathan's behavior, I didn't change my own. Couldn't I have stopped those walks to Harvard Square or postponed them? Couldn't I have gotten a babysitter?

Over the years I have squashed Jonathan back into that
stroller many times, not physically, but certainly metaphori-
cally. He and I were connected like the dancers inside the
domed glass of Grandma Plummer's music box, who are both
held together and kept apart by a thin, gold metal post. It
was our *fear* that bound and separated us. We could have used
a rehearsal.

Usually I don't dwell on regrets, but I want to make a
point with Jonathan today, want him to hear this from my
lips: I believe, Jonathan, that our parents in heaven share
absolutely none of the foibles of their human counterparts. I
believe that Heavenly Father will never give you stones when
you ask for bread, or serpents when you ask for fish. I believe
that He will never squash you down but will, instead, lift you
up to Himself and bless you.

In Matthew it says that Father in Heaven gives "good
things to them that ask him" (7:11). You were promised a
whole list of good gifts by the patriarch last week. This mission
call to Dearborn, Michigan, is a good gift.

You are yourself a good gift, Jonathan. In Mark it says,
"And he took a child, and set him in the midst of them: and
when he had taken him in his arms, he said unto them,
Whosoever shall receive one of such children in my name,
receiveth me: and whosoever shall receive me, receiveth not
me, but him that sent me" (9:36–37). I repeat, Jonathan, you
are a good gift to me and to your father.

I believe the atonement of Christ means that He —
Christ — will fill in the gaps of our sometimes disappointing
and half-failed relationships.

I believe what the poet said is absolutely true: "Above the

tent of stars, a loving father must dwell" (Friedrich Schiller, "Ode to Joy").

Strengthening the Family

When Tom and I had been married twenty years, we sent a Christmas card to our friends that looked like a full-page ad in a glossy magazine — it's a flattering photograph of the two of us sitting in front of a seamless backdrop, Tom's arm dangling pleasantly around my shoulder. We are both smiling into the eye of the camera with the kind of confidence exuded by what *People Magazine* calls "power couples." At the top of the page, above our heads, the greeting reads: "Twenty Years of Wishing You Merry Christmas." And to the side, superimposed onto the photograph, there is a paragraph that reads: "Twenty years without a single disagreement. Twenty years with a song in our hearts and nightly candlelit dinners of lean meats, whole grains, fresh fruits and vegetables, and polyunsaturates. Twenty years of lucid thoughts, eloquent conversations, and constant good humor. Twenty years of love at home. Twenty years without lust or cellulite or losing a single hair. Twenty years of well-behaved children, housebroken pets, and humming automobiles. Twenty years of financial solvency,

Goethe's poetry, and taut muscles." Finally, at the bottom of the picture, it says, "If you believe this, we have a river to sell you. Send twenty dollars to cover postage and handling for our free brochure. And Merry Christmas!"

In this Christmas greeting we presented an ideal of the two of us, and of our family, that we knew was false and, of course, so did our friends. The ideal we suggested was too outrageous to take seriously. And our friends responded by sending us Monopoly money, Venezuelan money, and Mexican coins. Our dentist, who could well afford it, sent us a check for twenty dollars that we pasted into our scrapbook.

But there is a side of us that wants to believe in this romantic ideal — that somewhere, somehow, perfect people are living perfect lives.

After I was asked to give this talk, I asked ten women, married and single, this question: "If you saw the title 'Strengthening the Family' in the printed program for stake conference, what would you expect to hear from the speaker?" Without exception each said, "Pray, read the scriptures, and hold regular family home evenings." What interested me most was the *way* they said it: with mild sneers at the corners of their lips. One woman added in a conspiratorial whisper, "all those things that don't work."

What is this cynicism about? Are prayer, scripture study, and family home evening just an ideal, outrageous like the Christmas card presentation of Tom and me and our family? Are they a joke?

Years ago, when our family was young and we had two small boys a year apart, we held weekly family home evenings. We had a scripture story, an activity, refreshments, and a prayer. In fact, our two young boys learned to say public prayers at those home evenings. In our enthusiasm to encourage this habit, Tom and I would clap and say, "Yeah!" after the amen when one of these toddlers could say a whole prayer by himself. But then one night in sacrament meeting in a new ward, where we were sitting in the back, both boys clapped and shouted, "Yeah!" after the opening prayer, and we knew we had to restrain some of our enthusiasm. Nevertheless, these were family home evenings we could feel good about. They were ideal.

But later, when one of our boys began boycotting family home evening, or worse, sabotaging it with cruel remarks or violent behavior that could not easily be ignored, our family home evenings were not so ideal. When he began clanking his plate with his fork during the prayer at dinner to show his opposition to us and to prayer alike, prayer for our family did not seem so ideal.

And later, one sunny afternoon in Saint Paul, Minnesota, that same boy lunged at me, grasped me around the throat in a headlock, pulled me to the floor, and said, strangling me, "Don't tell me what to do, or I'll kill you. Do you hear me? I'll kill you." And he tightened his grip. I believed he would kill me. I relaxed my whole body, went limp, and let him threaten me until his energies wore out. Then I said, "Let go of me now." And, finally, he did.

That afternoon, even now, stands out as the most humiliating day of my life. I was a mother abused by her son. I had been a good girl all my life. I had earned all the individual awards. I had had three years of perfect attendance in Mutual, sacrament, and Sunday School meetings. I loved the Book of

Mormon. I loved my parents. I never made out with boys. I did well in school. I used my talents. I said my prayers every day. I paid my tithing. I was a good girl. I didn't deserve to have a mean son. And I raged metaphorical fists at God. "Why me?" was my repeated question. And the answer was always the same: "Why not you?"

I left the house that afternoon and intended never to come back. I checked money out of the bank. And then I sat through two different movies by myself, bawling silently. I did not want to be the mother of this son. I seriously considered taking a Greyhound bus to the middle of South Dakota to spend the rest of my life working as a waitress in an inconspicuous diner. Let Tom take care of this, I thought.

Sometimes living in a family means suffering.

This is hard to believe on Sundays when we see each other smiling, articulate, organized, wearing clothes from Nordstrom, wearing Gucci watches. It is hard to believe that other people are suffering in their families when teachers giving lessons about abuse or drug addiction or chastity say, "Of course this isn't a problem in our ward, in our stake," a phrase I have heard more than once in the last five years, not just in lessons but in welfare meetings as well. It is a phrase that disturbs me deeply. I think of the baffled, pained, and vulnerable woman I was twelve years ago, and I know that if I had heard someone at church say that there is no family violence, no abuse in our ward, in our stake, I would have felt like I no longer belonged in this Church, where perfection seemed to be a fact. Not an ideal, but a fact.

The truth, I know now, is that a peaceful, loving, Mormon family is an ideal. The statistics bear this out. About half of first marriages in the Church end in divorce before the partners reach age sixty (Kristen L. Goodman and Tim B. Heaton, "LDS Church Members in the U.S. and Canada: A Demographic Profile," AMCAP *Journal* 12.1 [1986]: 92). It doesn't take much imagination to realize the suffering that both precedes and follows those divorces.

A recent Ann Landers column reported that 68 percent of Americans, asked if they would have children again if they had it to do over, said no.

And for that matter, only 38 percent of Church members even live in a "traditional family," with two parents and children. The rest are single, single parents, widows, and widowers (Goodman and Heaton, p. 96).

How do we strengthen our families, so diverse and so far from ideal?

Sometimes, when every cell inside us wants to leave and become a waitress in South Dakota, we go home and try again.

Sometimes, on the other hand, strengthening the family means leaving.

Sometimes we get help. The Church Social Services exists to help perfect the Saints. It does not exist because they are already perfect.

Sometimes we make our own family — like my friend Jane, who at age forty realized that she would never marry and then adopted two children.

Sometimes we remain single and make friends our family.

Sometimes, like a Native American woman I saw in front of Provo Bakery, we eat a lunch of sweet rolls and pop with our two little children while sitting on the curb, our legs stretching pleasantly into the street.

Sometimes we eat dinner around the table, and sometimes
we eat dinner in front of the TV and watch *Wheel of Fortune*.

I believe I know why those ten women answered, "Pray,
read the scriptures, and hold family home evenings" with
varying degrees of cynicism. It is because they have all had
times in their lives when that model didn't work. The good
news is that nothing stays the same. My son, who was so angry
growing up, has come to terms with his anger and is now
himself a remarkably responsible parent — something I never
would have imagined twelve years ago.

Families change. I realized in preparing this talk that I
avoided family home evening for years, because I had made
an emotional epic out of a few bad experiences. But my eleven-
year-old son wants to have it, and I am ready to try again.

And how do we strengthen our *stake* family? First, I think
we cannot hide behind a pretense of perfection. This is a
wonderful stake — the best I've ever lived in, in fact — but it
does have problems of abuse, family violence, adultery, AIDS,
bulimia, and loneliness. To pretend these problems don't exist
in our stake family is to isolate ourselves from each other.

Second, I think we should share our stories and not hide
them, hugger-mugger, from each other. If we tell our stories,
others will feel free to tell theirs without fear of judgment or
condescension. Sharing stories with each other gives us the
strength to move on.

I know in the past I have said that, like that 68 percent,
I would not have children again if I had it to do over, but I
have changed my mind. I want what God has promised me:
worlds without end — preferably well spaced — but I want them,
knowing full well that one-third of my own spirit children will

not share my values and will follow their own dark, solitary paths.

I believe that we are all God's "workmanship," as Paul says, "created in Christ Jesus unto good works" (Ephesians 2:10) and that through his divine grace and through faith, families as well as individuals can be made whole. This is my strength.

A Kissy Kissy
Christmas

It was the Christmas when I liked Ike. He had just won his second presidential election, and he and Mamie grinned at us from the cover of *Life* magazine. It was a Christmas of Perry Como and Bing Crosby specials; and the regulars, Russell Arms and Snookie Lanson and all the *Hit Parade* singers and dancers, still entertained us on Saturday nights. We hardly ever listened to the radio anymore. That Christmas I played my hi-fi, but instead of Christmas carols, I played "Your Kisses Take Me to Shangrila" by the Four Coins until the record grooves wore out. That Christmas I was fourteen, and I wanted to be kissed more than I wanted to breathe.

Don't get me wrong. I didn't want to be kissed by just anyone. I wanted to be kissed by *him. One and Only*. I hadn't met him, but I knew that when I did, our "eyes would lock forever," an expression I found in *The Ladies' Home Journal*. I didn't want him simply to kiss and run, or worse, kiss and tell. I wanted him to declare his love, marry me, and carry me away to the Forbushes' basement apartment, conveniently located across the back alley behind my parents' house. I would then exchange recipes with my mother and save crossword puzzles for my father. Mother and Dad would see that he was making me blissfully happy, and so there would be no need for them to worry about their fourteen-year-old married daughter.

That Christmas I spent part of my allowance on a sprig of mistletoe wrapped in cellophane with a meager red ribbon tied to the stem. I hung it on my bedroom wall above the half-dozen pictures of Tab Hunter carefully pasted above my bed. Tab Hunter with a redhead. Tab Hunter with a blonde. Tab Hunter with a brunette. The caption insisted he liked all types of girls as long as they had a nice sense of humor (which was about all I had to recommend me at age fourteen). Tab Hunter with his horses. Tab Hunter on Malibu Beach. Tab Hunter with his mother. Tab Hunter never kissed a girl on the first date. I respected Tab Hunter. I loved Tab Hunter. He would have been my first choice for kissing, marrying, and settling down in the Forbushes' apartment. But I knew reality from fantasy. He was just a picture on the wall. I needed someone real with real lips.

The real lips turned out to belong to Derek Scofield, whose parents owned the rest home on 9th East. He was three years older than I, and he *belonged* to my friend and next door neighbor, Myrna Kitchner. Actually, he was her interim boyfriend. She had gone all of her life with Leroy Bench, whom she eventually married; but that Christmas there had been a serious schism of sorts, and now Derek Scofield, who had a murky resemblance to Rock Hudson, was her boyfriend. Myrna revealed to me in hushed secrecy that he was a good kisser. The concept that kissing could be evaluated as good or bad was new to me; nevertheless, I was impressed. Because of Derek

Scofield, Myrna was the only one of my friends who sat in the Emigration Ward show with a boy.

One doesn't hear much about ward shows anymore, but in those days the Friday night ward shows were a significant part of my social life. I never missed them, and neither did my friends. My father, who was the elders quorum president, was responsible for choosing the films and running the projector. He had ordered for that particular Christmas season *Miracle on 34th Street* from the film catalog that we luckily got to keep at our house. But what arrived were two reels of *Miracle* and a third reel of some other movie, a cowboy movie, that had absolutely nothing to do with Christmas or miracles. Frustrated, my father called the distributors, who were apologetic but were unable to set things right, so instead of *Miracle on 34th Street,* we received a movie that had nothing to do with Christmas but that starred Fernando Lamas and Esther Williams. For me, at fourteen, this was better than *Miracle on 34th Street.* For one thing, Esther Williams was one of my favorite movie stars, and for another, I knew that she and Fernando Lamas would be kissing a lot. And, theoretically, I liked kissing. Besides, I'd already seen *Miracle on 34th Street* a dozen times.

So it was with a whole lot of anticipation that I stepped out of my front door that Friday night to attend the ward show. The first thing I saw was a light snow falling, a sign that life really did follow romantic song lyrics, because I *had* been dreaming of a white Christmas. Now it seemed a real possibility. The second thing I saw was Myrna standing on her porch with Derek. I could tell by their bent postures that she was sulking and he was placating her.

"What did I do?" he asked.

She leaned against the screen door, silent.

"Hi," I called over. "Are you guys going to the ward show?"

They stared at me as if I were a talking tree. Then, at the same time, he said yes and she said no.

"I don't want to go," she said, heaving an enormous sigh. "I don't feel good."

"Come on," he begged.

"No. Why don't you go with Louise?"

His head turned and considered me briefly. Like Belshazzar, I must have been weighed in the balance and found wanting, for he turned back to Myrna and begged again. "Pleeeze," he said.

She shook her head.

Then, to my surprise, Derek Scofield said he thought he *would* go with me and walked down the porch steps. When he reached the sidewalk, he swivelled around to see if Myrna was going to call him back, but she was already inside the screen door. He waited until she disappeared into the house, until the front porch light blinked off. Then he shrugged his shoulders, buried his hands deep into the pockets of his car coat, and, almost passing me on the sidewalk, said, "Let's go."

I had never had any trouble talking to Derek Scofield when he was Myrna's date, but now that he was *my* date, even though it was by default, I grew tongue-tied. It wasn't that I had never dated before. I had been to two Junior Gold and Green Balls weighed down by corsages larger than my chest, but I hadn't been able to speak on those occasions either. In my mind dating was equated with romance, not friendship. I was pretty comfortable with friendships even with boys, but I needed a scriptwriter for romance.

We walked side by side in the snow, which was now sticking to the sidewalk. From my peripheral vision, I was pleased to see that Derek was several inches taller than I was and that he had a remarkable resemblance to Rock Hudson. They could have been brothers. He smelled of Aqua Velva aftershave. We walked up the driveway, wordlessly, and entered the church through the back door, went up the stairs into the foyer, where the Christmas tree stood with large, colored lights, red balls, and silver icicles meticulously hung by Sister Wannamaker, the custodian's wife.

As we entered the recreation hall, I searched for my friends, Joyce Archer and Mary Ellen Schricker, and was disappointed when I couldn't see them. What was the point of having a date at the ward show if none of your friends was there to see the event? My dad was threading film through the projector, and I walked over to him. Here was a man I could talk to. "Are we going to have a cartoon?" I asked. Dad looked up briefly and nodded. "Hi, Derek," he said. "Better sit down; we're ready to roll."

I followed Derek to the third row from the front. "Is this okay?" he asked. He actually spoke to me. I didn't like to sit up that far but would rather have had smallpox than object. Derek hung his arm casually on the back of my folding chair, and I wiped my sweaty palms onto my pedal pushers. The cartoon was about Mickey Mouse trying to decorate a Christmas tree, with Pluto getting in the way and ruining it all the time. I glanced sideways at Derek and saw his Adam's apple move up and down. He turned to me and offered me some Sen Sens. I didn't know if this was a hint about the state of my breath or if it was an offer of refreshment. I put the Sen Sens in my mouth. They left an aftertaste of soap.

The feature film began. I loved Esther Williams and wished that I could relax and enjoy the movie. It wasn't long before Esther, adorned with rubber flowers, was swimming underwater. I marvelled at the way she could smile without choking. She and Fernando Lamas were attracted to each other from the beginning of the movie. Their eyes were always locking. They were going to kiss soon. I could tell by the swelling violins in the background. Kissing scenes were usually my favorite, but now with Derek Scofield sitting next to me, I began to be embarrassed. I wished they wouldn't, but they did, and when they did, Derek Scofield reached over and kissed me. On the mouth. I was too surprised to remember to close my eyes. I saw his two eyes become one. I saw individual hairs of his eyebrows and the pores of his skin. I smelled Aqua Velva and Sen Sens. But I felt nothing. Derek Scofield did not take me to Shangrila.

I immediately became a philosopher. Why had he kissed me, I asked myself. He hardly knew me. I wasn't his girlfriend; Myrna was. Shouldn't we talk first and then kiss? I desperately wished he would lean over and say something funny, something hilarious. I wanted to laugh. I, silly girl, wanted a reason for his kissing me.

The violins were building up to another kissing scene. Apparently, the first kiss had merely whetted Fernando Lamas's Latin appetite. This time he Crushed Esther Williams to Him Passionately. Derek Scofield lurched from his chair and grabbed me so awkwardly and violently that I thought my folding chair would collapse. His kiss was wet and slightly off center. He had both arms clasped tightly around me, and the only thing that prevented my being completely engulfed was my handbag, which I clutched against my chest like a shield. His buttons pressed into my arm. I held my breath until it was over. My neck was sore when I leaned back in my chair.

I decided some things. I decided Derek Scofield's hormones were triggered by what he saw, and what he saw was Fernando Lamas and Esther Williams kissing. When they did, he did. I decided he would have kissed Eleanor Roosevelt just as violently if she had been sitting next to him. That being the case, I decided that Derek Scofield had kissed me for the last time.

Having seen a hundred similar movies, I knew there would be more kissing scenes than I could deal with. How could I tell him that I didn't want to be kissed anymore? I couldn't. I'd rather tell him I had to go to the bathroom, and I'd never do that.

Instead, I sat forward in my seat, both feet squarely planted on the floor, both elbows on my knees, and both hands clamped against my Sweetheart Pink mouth as if I had hoof-and-mouth disease. It was difficult watching the movie in that position. In fact, it was difficult breathing. My handbag guarded my chest.

Esther Williams and Fernando Lamas had the inevitable disagreement and then the inevitable making-up period, accompanied by much passionate kissing. I was glad I was prepared.

Derek Scofield leaned forward and asked, "What's the matter?"

"Nothing," I mumbled from behind my hands.

"Why have you got your hands on your mouth?" Suddenly he wanted to communicate. "Are you sick?"

I shook my head. He wouldn't see my mouth again while I lived.

He slumped back in his seat.

When the movie was over, we walked home as we had come, without speaking. The kissing and marriage fantasies of that Christmas season washed over me like waves of nausea. Tab Hunter made me sick. The Four Coins made me sick. Esther Williams and Fernando Lamas made me sick. Mostly I, Louise Roos, with my delusions of romantic grandeur, made myself sick. I wanted to throw up.

By the time Christmas rolled around about a week and a half later, I had already thrown the pictures of Tab Hunter away as well as the mistletoe. I threw away "Your Kisses Take Me to Shangrila." I didn't kiss again until I was twenty years old and dating the man who would be my husband. He talked to me (and I talked back), and he made me laugh, and laughter, as it turns out, is the best aphrodisiac of all.

The Fourth of July

The fourth of July creates a confusion of loyalties for me. Because I was born in the Netherlands and have Dutch parents, I am a lifelong citizen of that country, even though I only spent five and a half years living there. My parents immigrated to America in 1948 with four children (I was the oldest). In 1953 they were sworn in as American citizens, and their children became naturalized citizens. So I am a citizen of two countries: Holland and America.

To be Dutch means you have ancestors with wonderful guttural names, like Lodewijk and Geertje Roos. Like Jan and Jannigje Copier. Like Jan deWith and Trijntje van Rinsum. Like Howard Van Fleet. Like Jan van Ginkel and Pieternella Bardie. And my favorite, Neeltje van de Verguldenbijl.

These people came from places like Breukelen, Utrecht, Achtien Hoven, Dordrecht, and Oudewater.

For a long time, being Dutch meant thinking that all mothers ironed their children's underwear and scrubbed the sidewalk in front of their houses every Friday afternoon.

To be Dutch meant watching Mother deep-frying *oliebollen*

and *appelflappen* on New Year's Eve and fighting over who got to sift the powdered sugar on the finished ones.

Being Dutch meant your friends were always exclaiming, "Your parents have an accent!" And my own children, who are less tactful, asking, "How come they talk funny?"

I have been back to Holland and have felt quite at home. Sometimes I have missed not being able to grow up there. I have missed the city where I was born, Utrecht, which is two thousand years old, with its gabled houses, cobbled streets, canals, organ grinders, and flower vendors. I have missed the rich cultural surrounding bestowed by Rembrandt, Vermeer, and Van Gogh. I miss Breukelen, with its peaceful green landscape, the lovely River Vecht edged with stately homes, the village, the locks and bridges, the black and white cows, the buttercups that grow along the paths. I miss Opoe and Opa's (my grandparents') house, which is now gone forever. I miss the seashore. I miss the windmills. I think of it as a land of jewels.

Why would anyone want to leave such a country?

Last Sunday night, Tom and I visited my parents, as we often do on Sunday evenings. I wanted to ask them why they left Holland to live in America. When we arrived, they were watching Perry Mason. It reminded me of the time I visited Holland with the two of them a few years ago. We stayed with my father's brother, Dick, and his wife, Dien. The television ran old American TV shows in English with Dutch subtitles. My uncle Dick liked *Perry Mason* especially. When Raymond Burr appeared, my uncle exclaimed, "Oh, this is a very good show. Do they have this in America?" My parents and I tittered politely. Yes, we'd seen it about a thousand

times, a thousand years ago. He repeated this question when
Gunsmoke came on: "Do they have this in America?" My
father tells him yes, and when he's not looking, rolls his eyes
back in his head for my mother and me to see. This little TV
ritual continues with *Mannix* and *Hawaii Five-0*, my father
growing increasingly irritated with his brother's naive questions. When Uncle Dick asks if we have *I Love Lucy* in America, my father explodes with "It's *made* in America! Can't you
hear? They're speaking English!"

My uncle Dick puffs on his cigar. "They could have been
BBC productions," he suggests calmly.

Perhaps my father and mother left Holland to get away
from such relatives.

I ask them as they are watching the new Perry Mason,
"Why did you come to America? Holland seems like a pretty
good country to me. Why leave?"

"America is better in every way," my father says.

I don't like this vague answer, and I push them a little
harder.

"The war was awful, and after the war you couldn't get
anything," my mother says.

"We wanted to go to Zion," explains my father. "We had
four children, and we wanted to be sealed in the temple. And
there was no temple in Europe then. The Swiss temple was
built seven years after we came to America. We didn't know
if there would ever be a temple in Europe."

"But I thought you wanted to come to America even before
the war, before you joined the Church," I say to my father.

"Well, yes," he says. "I wanted to leave. I almost went
to the East Indies with a friend."

My father was sounding more and more like Christopher Columbus—heading for the East Indies and ending up in America by mistake.

"But what is it about America, precisely?" I ask. "You've been back to Holland many times. What is it about America that you like so much?"

He can see that I am disappointed with his answers. "It just feels freer here," he says.

"You can feel it in the air," my mother says.

"People feel more equal here," my father says.

He tells how amazed he was the first time he went to the doctor. "He spoke to me like a real human being," he says. "You can have goals in America and actually expect to make them. You can start out poor and end up rich." He chuckles, "Or at least middle class. You can't do that in Holland."

They go on and tell about how they bought a car the first three months they were here. Dick, his brother in Holland, wasn't able to buy a car until the mid 1970s.

They bought a house the second year they were here. Dick wasn't able to buy a house until about the time he bought the car—again, in the mid seventies.

They talk about the convenience of America, the space, adult education, and appliances.

Often I fantasize: what if we had never come to America, and I had grown up in Utrecht?

Well, I would probably ice-skate better than I do now.

And I would have married some other man who would also make me laugh. It is unlikely, my father tells me, that as an electrician's daughter I would have married a professor's son as I did.

My father got tired of my asking him questions. "Don't you like America?" he asks me.

"Of course," I say.

"Well, what do *you* like about it?"

I can only think of vague, meaningless clichés — it is the land of the free and the home of the brave, blah, blah, blah — I am as stuck for an answer as he was earlier. It is only later, when I am alone, that I know why I love America.

Years ago Tom and I and our two oldest sons spent a sabbatical year in West Berlin. It was a pleasant year. We had good housing, good food, good transportation, friends, entertaining outings. It was all very swell. When we arrived in Chicago, I wanted to kiss the ground. When I got home to Minneapolis, I walked directly to the basement and kissed my washing machine, which was much more efficient than the German washer.

My friend Ginny Wirthlin said she too wanted to kiss the ground in New York when she returned from a wonderful year in London. My father always wants to kiss the Statue of Liberty when he returns from Holland.

What is that all about? Is it just because it's home? In part, I think it is. But like my father, I think America *feels different*. It has a spirit and energy that to me is uniquely American. It is a kind of optimism, a belief in dreams, miracles, and happy endings.

The spirit of America for me is reflected in its diverse talents from Thomas Jefferson to George Gershwin, from Thomas Alva Edison to Shirley Temple, from E.B. White to Erma Bombeck, from Garrison Keillor to Woody Allen, from the Reverend Norman Vincent Peale to the Reverend Martin Luther King.

The spirit of America is reflected in its diverse cities: New York, Houston, New Orleans, Seattle, Detroit, Chicago, Minneapolis, and Hollywood.

The spirit of America is reflected in its diverse language — its black rap, its Texas drawl, its Brooklyn twang, its California surfer.

How could I *not* read, write, and sing in English?

How could I not be immersed in American humor — its Johnny jokes, its knock-knock jokes, and its what's-grosser-than-gross jokes? How could I not understand the jokes of American Indians about Custer and Columbus? "Did you hear that Custer was well dressed when he died? He was wearing an arrow shirt." Or, "What did the Indians say when the Pilgrims landed?" "Well, there goes the neighborhood."

How could I not enjoy the way Americans advertise their personalities on their chests and car bumpers: "If you don't like the way I'm driving, get off the sidewalk," or, "I refuse to have a battle of wits with an unarmed person," or, "Body by Nautilus, brain by Mattell."

How could I not love America's Jell-O salads with marshmallows, its chocolate-chip cookies, the 1958 Chevy Impala, Kool-Aid, Kermit the Frog, Mickey Mouse, Mickey Mantle, and Teen-Age Mutant Ninja Turtles. How could I not love the jump-rope rhymes of my early childhood in America:

> *Postman, postman do your duty,*
> *Here comes Louise, an American beauty.*
> *She can wiggle, she can waggle, she can do the splits,*
> *She can wear her dresses up above her hips.*

How could I not love the lines of American writers that

I have read in my adult years? The paradoxes of Emily Dickinson: "I heard a fly buzz when I died." The simple truths of Robert Frost: "Good fences make good neighbors." And how could I not love the unrestrained forthrightness of the poet Lucille Clifton paying homage to her hips?

> *these hips are big hips.*
> *they need space to*
> *move around in.*
> *they don't fit into little*
> *petty places. these hips*
> *are free hips.*

("*Homage to My Hips*," two-headed woman [Amherst: University of Massachusetts Press, 1980], 6)

It is the free, uninhibited spirit of America that I love, an America that has allowed me my own dreams. As a child I dreamed of being a Dutch princess and wearing white every day. Later I wanted to be an artist and live on Monhegan Island off the coast of Maine. Then I wanted to live in New York City as a fashion illustrator. I wanted to be a movie star in Hollywood, chauffeured around town in a limousine. I wanted to study English literature and become a writer or a teacher.

Now I realize that in America I am better than a princess or a movie star. I am free to go where I please, when I please. I can ride the bus. I can cross state lines. I can wear white every day of my life. But like Bartleby the Scrivener, I would prefer not to.

I sing America. America the beautiful. I sing from sea to shining sea.

Wallflower

Yes, I look good. I look really great, as a matter of fact. I needn't worry about anything. I look sensational in this red dress. Red looks best on me, and I look sensational. Except for the buttons. I don't like the buttons Mother picked. They're really crummy buttons. But if I hold my arm up in front like this, no one will see them there. Now I really do look sensational, and no one can see the buttons at all. I feel the music. I'm with it. It's going to work for me tonight. Positive thinking will work. It will. It will.

There's Herb Blakely. He's looking at me. He likes my dress. I can tell. He took a step toward me. I'll bet he wants to dance with me, but he's afraid to ask. I'll smile at him. Come across the room, Herbie, and ask me to dance. Tell me I look sensational. Ask me to dance, Herbie. The power of positive thinking is at work. Ask me, Herbie. Ask me.

You jerk! He'll be back, maybe. I'm sure he looked at me. Herbie likes me. He said hi in Sunday School last week. That's all he said, but I could tell by the way he said it that he likes me. He said hi and then walked past me. But I could tell it meant something.

If I don't stand by any other girls, someone will ask me to dance. Oh my gosh, here comes Martha Bluke. Go away, Martha. Go away. Don't stand here by me. Go away, Martha. The power of positive thinking. It worked. I can't believe it. She went over to the corner with Mary Anne Little and Beth Kelly. They're dancing with each other! Oh, I can't stand it. Three girls dancing in a corner. It's disgusting. I can't stand it. I think I'm going to die right on the spot.

Oh, there's Ralph. I'll smile a little more. He is so darling. Really. He is really so very cool. He looked at me. My mouth hurts from smiling and my arm hurts too. Crummy buttons. Tell me I'm witty and cute, Ralph. Oh, Ralph, you could make my entire adolescence if you'd just ask me to dance. Ask me, Ralph. Ask me. He asked Lila Kirk. Jerk. Look how close they're dancing. Isn't anyone going to break them up? I would never dance that close with anyone. Not with anyone.

Except maybe Chuck Stewart. I just adore him. He is so neat. He always stands with his hands in his pockets. I really like that. And his hair touches his ears in a really groovy way, and I think he shaves. I'll bet he's the only boy in this entire ward who shaves. There he is. Oh, I can't breathe. If I could dance with Chuck Stewart I'd never ask for another thing in my entire life. I'm smiling at him, and I've got all my buttons covered, and he's looking at me.

I winked at him! How could I wink at him? It was an accident. I winked at Chuck Stewart. I must have a tic. I must. I've never in my life done that. He'll think I'm a flirt. Oh Chuck, I didn't mean to wink at you like a creep. He asked Martha. Martha! How could he ask her? She was dancing with all those girls and he asked her. It was because I winked,

I'll bet. He'd rather ask a girl who dances with girls than a girl who winks. I must have a tic. Martha thinks she dances so well. She doesn't.

Roger Humphries! I thought he'd moved out of the ward. Oh wow! Oh neato! Look at the way he chews his gum. I'm going to die. Right now. I'm going to die. He's walking across the dance floor. Oh, I can't breathe. My arm is going to sleep. Positive thinking. Positive thinking. Ask me — ask me — ask me. Oh Roger, you are so *numero uno* neato! He's looking at me. My lips are quivering. They're quivering. My palms are beginning to perspire. It's not ladylike. He's coming right toward me. Oh my mouth hurts. My arm. My crummy buttons. Why didn't I wear something else? Ask me, Roger. Ask me to dance, Roger. Tell me I'm the best looking thing you've seen all night. Tell me I'm beautiful and charming and witty and exciting and that you've had your eye on me for years. Tell me you love me, Roger. Or just ask me to dance!

Don't walk past me. He's drinking red punch. Red punch! Why not red dress? Me? Oh pooh, who cares? I don't. I really don't. To think I came to this duddy dance when I could be home reading *The Scarlet Letter*.

My father! My father the bishop is walking toward me. No, Daddy, no. No. Please don't. Please go to the punch bowl. No, Daddy, don't smile so lovingly at me. Oh, please let me be struck dead instantly. He says I'm the most beautiful thing he's seen all evening. Would I dance just one with him? He says I'm exciting and charming and witty and that I dance like Ginger Rogers, whoever she is. He says he loves me.

Oh, Daddy, I love you too.

FEAR, I EMBRACE YOU

All my life I have been a dreamer. In my first dream, I wanted to be the queen of Holland's daughter. Not the oldest one, Beatrix, who is now herself the queen and who always reminded me of a plump squirrel with nuts stored solidly in its cheeks. Nor did I want to be the youngest daughter, the one with cross-eyes — I forget her name. I wanted to be Marijka, the second daughter, who was my age and fair and lovely as a princess ought to be. She wore her hair parted on the left side with a generous white taffeta bow on the right. In fact, all her clothes were white: white socks with white shoes, white dresses with white lace trim. She was clean enough to be translated.

I looked like the immigrant girl that I was. I wore Buster Brown oxfords with brown laces and cable-knit knee socks.

When this dream was used up, I replaced it with another dream. I dreamed of a family: a mother named Sally, a father named Jim, and a beautiful eight-year-old girl, who was me, only her blonde hair was naturally curly and her name was Betsy, not Louise. Not surprisingly, the family of my dream always dressed in white and never got dirty. Their world was the perfectly sunny world of the impressionists. Betsy wore a taffeta ribbon in her hair and walked between her parents holding their hands when they weren't all three riding in their white Packard convertible with the shiny chrome bumpers.

In reality, when I was eight years old, I was the oldest of five children, and I still wore those Buster Brown oxfords with the brown laces and the cable-knit knee socks. My father drove a 1936 Ford sedan.

In seventh grade, I dreamed that I dressed every day in the same dance outfit: a short, black taffeta skirt and a white silk blouse with enormous butterfly sleeves and black patent leather tap shoes. I tap-danced my way into the heart of every other seventh grader and became the most popular girl at Hamilton School because I was a star.

In reality, I had plenty of friends, but I wasn't the most popular girl in school. Diana Mitchell was. I wore Joyce shoes imitations from Baker's.

In junior high school, I wanted to be an actress. In high school, I wanted to be an artist or a writer. All my life I have dreamed dreams of being transformed into someone popular as Diana Mitchell, beautiful as Grace Kelly, talented as Georgia O'Keefe, and smart as Margaret Mead. I wanted to soar like some mythical bird with gauzy wings and spell my name — Louise — with my white breath across the sky while ordinary mortals stared up at me in awe, calling my name, pleading for my autograph from the sidewalk below.

These dreams were my vision of a creative life. For me, being a creative person means to make a mark in the world. It is "the act of making something new, whether a symphony, a novel, an improved layout for a supermarket, [or] a new and unexpected casserole dish" (S.I. Hayakawa, "What Does It Mean to Be Creative?" *Through the Communication Barrier: On Speaking, Listening, and Understanding*, ed. Arthur Chandler [New York: Harper and Row, 1979], 106).

My question is, What keeps us from making our mark?

One of my favorite stories from Greek mythology is the story of the boy Icarus. He and his father, Daedalus, were held prisoners inside a labyrinth on the island of Crete by King Minos. Max J. Herzberg tells us that in order to escape, Daedalus "devised a pair of wings for himself and a pair for Icarus. He fastened them to his own shoulders and those of the boy, using wax as the binding material. Then both triumphantly flew away. Swiftly they skimmed through the air, and closer and closer they came to the mainland. But Icarus, flushed with excitement and exhilaration, soared even higher toward the sun — despite the warnings of his father. At last, he flew so high that the heat of the sun melted the wax, and off dropped the wings. The lad plunged downward into the sea and was drowned" (*Myths and Their Meaning* [Boston: Allyn and Bacon, 1953], 56).

The Icarus myth is frequently alluded to by artists and poets. Brueghel, in his painting *The Fall of Icarus*, shows a tiny pair of white legs protruding from the ocean just short of the coastline in the lower right corner of the canvas. Most poets focus on the failure of Icarus — his fall from the sky. Anne Sexton, however, in her poem, "To a Friend Whose Work Has Come to Triumph," focuses on the exhilaration of the flight and not the fall. She writes:

Consider Icarus, pasting those sticky wings on,

testing that strange little tug at his shoulder blade,
and think of that first flawless moment over the lawn
of the labyrinth. Think of the difference it made!
There below are the trees, as awkward as camels;
and here are the shocked starlings pumping past
and think of innocent Icarus who is doing quite well:
larger than a sail, over the fog and the blast
of the plushy ocean, he goes. Admire his wings!
Feel the fire at his neck and see how casually
he glances up and is caught, wondrously tunneling
into that hot eye. Who cares that he fell back to the sea?
See him acclaiming the sun and come plunging down
while his sensible daddy goes straight into town.
(The Complete Poems [*Boston: Houghton Mifflin, 1981*], 53)

Most of Sexton's poem concentrates not only on the thrill of the flight but also on its success: "See him acclaiming the sun," she writes. She is not, it seems to me, applauding the safe, "sensible daddy."

Flight, in literature, is often a figurative expression of creativity. The paradox is that the flight is both exhilarating and life-threatening. In real life, the metaphor also holds true. There is always the danger in creating anything, in taking flight, that like Icarus, we could fall from the sky and die.

I used to say to my mother, "I'm going to marry a rich man. I want to travel all over Europe. I'm going to be an actress. I want to be an artist. I want to live in New York City. I want to be a writer. I'm going to be famous some day."

My mother's reply was, "Pff." Just a little explosion of air through the lips. "Pff." It meant a myriad of things like, "You're crazy. Don't get your hopes up. Life is harder than you can imagine. Things don't work out so simply. No one I know is an artist, a writer, or an actress. No one I know married a rich man. What you want may not be possible. Pff. Pff."

I don't blame my mother. It was her job, I now realize, to be sensible, to steer me away from that brilliant sun before my wax melted.

My own sons have dreams, and they are not my dreams. To tell you the truth, I want every one of them to be English professors. That would make me happy, if they all became English professors. After high school, my second son, Ed, signed up with BYU's Air Force ROTC and was allowed to join student pilots in those little planes, the size of cars, and fly above Provo. The first time he did that, he flew by our balcony and had the pilot tip the wings of the plane at us. That was friendly, and I liked it. I liked Ed's enthusiasm too, but then he began talking about flying F-16s and doing stalls and barrel rolls. Like Daedalus, I began to see the danger. From then on, it made me cringe when Ed, in his most exuberant, unique voice would say, "I'm gonna fly F-16s. It's gonna be so cool. I'm gonna be Top Gun."

And even though I've fought this attitude all my life, I say "Pff." Because that creative dream that he has for himself, his own expression of self, is not one that I know — is not one that seems possible to me. It scares me, just like my dreams scared my mother. I'm afraid that boy is going to melt his wax and fall into Utah Lake.

I repeat my question: What keeps us from making our mark in the world? I think it is fear. Fear that stems from repeated warnings we have received from loving, well-meaning, "sensible daddies and mommies" who want to keep us safe and who are themselves afraid. In Shakespeare's *Hamlet*, Laertes warns his sister, Ophelia, against Hamlet's advances with this dictum: "The best safety is fear" (1.3.43).

Here I am faced with that paradox again of taking risks that lead to creative expression versus safety. In my son's case, the risks are real. He could, like Icarus, literally fall out of the sky and die, but he claims the flight is worth the risk. But I have come to realize that for most of the rest of us, becoming the self we dream of being, the self who can make a joyful mark on the world, means taking a risk that only *feels* life-threatening. It only *feels* as if we're falling out of the sky. The risk is not death but disapproval from family and friends. The risk is becoming the butt of the joke. Failure and humiliation are the real risks, and humiliation feels as scary as drowning.

I know this from my own experience. From my adolescent journals two tasks emerge again and again: drawing and writing. I think I was clearer on what I was about as a teenager than I was in my thirties: drawing and writing were my work. But I became afraid of that work.

When I was nineteen years old and attending the University of Utah, I changed my major about as often as I changed my underwear. One day, I was an art major. I took Basic Drawing in a barracks on the east side of campus. I sat in front of an easel with a large sketch pad, a piece of charcoal that stained my fingers, and a gummy eraser that I could knead into a ball. I drew cylinders and globes lit from various angles. I drew the back of a sculptured male figure, shading the muscles. Whereas in high school I had received A's in art, at the university my drawings and my notebook received B-plusses.

That didn't bother me. I knew the competition would be stiffer at the university, and I was satisfied for the time being with the B-plusses. Logically, I should have received a B-plus in the class; however, my ability to draw was only part of the grade. I was also tested twice in a midterm and a final exam in which I was to identify the drawings of famous artists.

My art professor told us we could study the drawings in the Art Library. I went into that library just once, searching for books containing the drawings of the masters, but I didn't know how to find them. I couldn't see a card catalogue, and I suppose now that if I had, I wouldn't have known what to look for. There was a librarian behind the desk, but she was busy with other people. Besides, there was an efficient, brusque air about her that intimidated me. I was afraid that when I approached her, she would say, "Pff." So I did not ask for help, and because I didn't ask for help, I received a C in Basic Drawing — a grade of C for a subject that I had only excelled in before. The professor, in an end-of-the-class interview, told me I had a flair for fashion illustration, but I needed to apply myself more. I got a C in art, because I was too afraid to take a risk and ask a librarian for help.

The next day I changed my major to English. The first class I took was an Introduction to Literature. The professor was a slim, grayish man who wore black turtleneck sweaters and who sat cross-legged upon the desk in front of the room like an aging Hamlet. I thought he was part of the beat generation, sardonic, cynical, and witty in an arrogant sort of way. He spoke about literature with an eastern accent. Sometimes he smoked in class. For all of these reasons, I loved him. Naturally, I wanted to please him, but this was not to be. I had to write a paper on Ford Maddox Ford's novel *The Good Soldier*. I read the book on a train to San Francisco during the Thanksgiving holiday. I was clueless as to what the book was about. On Sunday night, coming back from San Francisco, I was still clueless — and in that state, I wrote the paper. After the papers were handed in, my professor began telling us about *The Good Soldier*. I was astonished to hear that the first person narrator was a *naive narrator,* a term I had never heard in my life, and that his view of what was going on around him was a *distortion.* I knew then that I had missed the whole point, and sure enough, when the papers were returned, I had received a C-, which was exactly what I deserved. There was no chance for revision. I felt humiliated. All that reading and writing I had done through childhood, through adolescence, was not good enough to save me in this class. I was too scared and too proud to ask the professor for help. He might, after all, say, "Pff." The next day I changed my major to child development.

I did not return to English literature until I was thirty years old with two babies and was thoroughly fed up with child developing. I took a class on the short story. My husband sat up with me the night before a three-page paper was due on Hawthorne's "My Kinsman Major Molineux." He practically moved the pencil while I hyperventilated. Not only did I get an A, but the professor read it aloud in class. So now I knew that my husband could write a good paper. Then I discovered the library — finally. When I was clueless about a text, I went to the library and borrowed others' ideas freely. I never again received a grade below A-. By the time I reached graduate school, I had learned how to write a paper by myself.

Because of my chronic fear, I am a classic late bloomer. I finished my undergraduate degree when I was thirty-seven years old. I wanted desperately to go to graduate school, but I almost didn't, because I was too afraid to ask three professors for letters of recommendation. I was afraid they wouldn't remember me, that they would give me vague looks and say, "Pff." Finally, a supportive friend, recognizing both my desire and my fear, said she would meet me at the library on a Thursday night and that I was to report to her that I had asked for the letters.

I did it. All three professors remembered me. No one laughed. I got into graduate school, and because I did, other dreams came true. I write, I teach, I even tap dance. Because I finally got the nerve to ask for three letters, I got a whole new life. (Although I am still waiting for all those white dresses to arrive.)

I am now forty-seven years old, and I am still afraid, but I've learned that to limit myself to safe activities because I'm too afraid to ask questions, or too afraid to take a class, or too afraid to ask for letters of recommendation, or to apply for a job, or give a talk or teach a lesson — to limit myself out of fear — is more like drowning in the ocean than confronting the fear itself. For me, it led to depression. Fear does not kill; it only gives you diarrhea. I have come to think of diarrhea as a friend who helps me lose weight. The really big fear makes me gag, or worse, throw up. I have lived through that too, and again, it's good for weight control. Fear, I have come to realize, is my companion for life, and I embrace her. Fear has become the force that drives my creative energy.

Finally, I find that when I am living the life I want to

live, I can allow others to live theirs. I don't need to control or manipulate them into fulfilling some dream that I can't fulfill for myself. I can live with Ed zooming through the sky, piloting his F-16. He really doesn't have to be an English professor for me.

I don't know if I can live with my younger son, Charles, though. He tests me sorely. "What do you want me to be when I grow up?" he asked me one day. I should have known it was a trap.

Generous spirited, I said, "I want you to be what you want to be."

"Well, then," he said, his eyes flashing at me, "I want to be a hit man."

LETTER TO
KATHRYN BLAKE

University of Minnesota
Minneapolis, Minnesota 55455
Friday, December 8, 1978

Dear Kathryn,

The Board of Regents' office is quiet as a pillow this morning. Everyone is at the Regents' meeting at the Earl Brown Center on the Saint Paul campus. That leaves me here alone with absolutely nothing to do except write letters. As you know, I don't write letters, and I *never* write my mother, nor does she ever write me. I don't think either one of us has spent half a minute feeling sorry about it. But since *you* write letters and no one ever writes you back, I thought I would write you even though you live just around the corner.

First, the weather: let me say that I haven't seen you strolling your dog the last several mornings. Does he become severely constipated in subzero temperatures? I find that on mornings like this morning, when the thermometer rises weakly to a minus 23 degrees, the hairs in my nose are frozen before I can cross the street, and tears stream involuntarily

81

down my face. I stand waiting for the bus, not reading the schedule again, and think "warm." It doesn't help. I have to wait for the bus exactly four minutes, except for this morning, when it was eight minutes late. My face was a mass of frozen body waters. It is tempting to buy one of those ski masks, except that I associate them with people who disguise themselves in order to commit heinous crimes. Ax murderers wear ski masks. Son of Sam probably wore one.

I know how to get a seat on the bus. I learned it from old women. You just keep your feet moving. No matter where I'm standing in a waiting crowd, if I keep my feet moving, I get on in time to get a seat. An important skill, I think.

Second, the children: you would lose all respect for me if you saw their bedrooms. Gerbils, hamsters, parakeets, and their individual doo-doos and food mixed in together. Torn books, dirty underwear, gum wrappers, melted M&M candies, and bowls of petrified ice cream. I tell you, it's disgusting. On the weekends, they clean up. This means they shove it all into a closet and vacuum the floor. During the week, it all finds its way back.

It is easier to talk about their environs — the children's, that is — than it is to talk about their psyches. I would like to say that their psyches are fine but, in fact, Edmund blubbers if he is left at home ten minutes without our saying where we're going. Yesterday I drove Tom to the university. The boys were up in their bedroom watching television, so Tom and I left quietly. When I returned, Edmund was blubbering on his bed. I use the word "blubbering," because it is exactly what he does. His lips go blubber blubber, and his face becomes juicy (a trait inherited from his mother, I guess). Anyway, I apologized to him, and he told me never to do it again. Jonathan kicks doors and threatens to bite his violin. I imagine he will buy one of those ski masks when he grows up. Charlie is spoiled rotten, and no one is doing anything about it, because he says cute things such as, "When I grow up, I want to marry my beautiful mother."

Third, the husband: He is a cookie, but there is strain between us. Our priorities are not the same. My number one priority is to get the confounded house finished. His priorities are to finish a report for the dean, to finish a grant proposal for the National Endowment for the Humanities, to have tithing settlement, and to correct eighty final exams. We have had these strains before, and they are not serious, only irritating. I am not having any secret fantasies about catching the next bus to New York City or anything. At least not this minute.

Fourth, the house: I hate the house!

Fifth, the mother-in-law: she is coming on Monday afternoon and will stay a month. The children adore her and ask every day when she is coming. We are not entirely ready (see irritation above), but I don't think she will mind as much as I mind. She will bring homemade raspberry jam and maybe homemade mincemeat cookies. I hope so. She will despise the cold weather.

I always recommend at least one book in the letters I don't write. The best book I've read this year was *Angle of Repose*, by Wallace Stegner. He won a Pulitzer Prize for it in 1972. Lovely writing and painful story. Right now I'm reading Lillian Hellman's *Scoundrel Time*, which tells of her experiences with the McCarthy era. Interesting. I am fascinated with Lillian Hellman anyway.

I am not going on to page three. Have a lovely day, my friend. You are such a cookie. And you owe me a letter!

Love,
Louise

THE
5-MINUTES-A-DAY
JOURNAL

I had two Dutch grandmothers: a city grandmother, who was called Oma, and a country grandmother, who was called Opoe. Opoe made great rounds of cheese that she kept in a cool cellar. She churned her own butter and gathered eggs from a hen house. Her meals were heavy on potatoes. On Sundays, she served everyone in her large family a piece of meat the size of a silver dollar along with the potatoes. After she joined the Church and read that meat was to be eaten sparingly, she cut down the size of that small portion of meat even further. My mother said that Opoe was afraid of Hell.

Oma lived in the city of Utrecht and always had a parakeet or two to fuss over. She liked sweets and kept cookies in a tin. At Christmas, she gave us marzipan candies shaped into fruits. I remember her as a rather eccentric, deaf old lady. When I visited her in Utrecht, she kept her television turned to an unbearable volume and then shouted over it. She picked the lint off my navy blue raincoat and said Americans didn't dress as tastefully as Dutch people. This from a woman whose living room walls were covered with souvenir plates from Salt Lake City. My father says that Oma, who couldn't swim, was afraid of water.

I have no idea what either one of these women was like as children, as teenagers or even as young mothers. What I know of them is what my parents tell me and what I have observed of them when they were already old women. Oma didn't write a word about herself, and Opoe wrote a couple of pages that summarized her entire life. Not very satisfying for a snoopy granddaughter.

What do I want from them? What do I want to know? I have made an incomplete list:

1. I would like to know what their daily routine was like. What time did they get up and when did they go to bed? Neither woman had a car. Did they shop daily? Did it take all day to do the laundry? How often did they change the sheets on their beds?

2. I would like to know what they ate. Just one week of menus would satisfy me on this score. Did they eat *oliebollen* and *appelflappen*? Did they eat *poffertjes*? Certainly not granola bars or Frankenberries. And I can say with certainty that they never called out for pizza.

3. What did they dream? What did they dream when asleep? When awake?

4. What were their wedding days like? Did they love their husbands? Did they stop loving their husbands?

5. What did they think about their own lives, their children, their homes? Were they satisfied with their furniture? With themselves?

I suspect that each grandmother thought her life ordinary,

commonplace, and routine. And yet the fabric of their "ordinary" lives was completely different from my own life. They fed chickens and canaries. I feed gerbils. They churned butter. I eat low cholesterol tub margarine. They had housemaid's knee; I have video wrist.

I wish they had written about themselves. I wish I could hear those two unique voices in their own writings, but I can't.

Many of us do not write about ourselves either, because we think our lives are boring. We don't appreciate the fabric of our own life, the details of it, the repetition of it. We don't understand that our experience as ordinary human beings is valuable. We don't understand that just by being alive we are unique. I wish my grandmothers had kept a journal. It is through the journal that we record our uniqueness.

Journal writing is relaxed writing. It is a book for which we make our own rules. I know people who write a page every night and people who write a "chapter" on Sunday afternoons, and I know people who carry their journals around with them and write in them during brief intervals in the day. Some people keep a journal for a year and skip three years and then begin another journal. And of course some people don't keep a journal at all. For some of us, writing anything at all is a tense experience. We are too aware of our deficiencies: either we feel dumb, or we can't spell, or it simply takes too much time.

I'd like to share a technique used by many professional writers called *rush writing* that addresses some of the stress we feel about writing. Rush writing is simply writing down your first thoughts. It is a timed writing. This is how you do it: You set a timer (I have an oven timer especially for writing) for a short time—five minutes is enough—and you write as fast as you can, never allowing your pen or pencil to leave the page. Keep your mind focused on the paper. If you hit a blank, then simply write, "I just hit a blank" and keep writing that until you think of something else to write. The main rule is to keep writing no matter what. When the bell rings, finish your sentence and quit. You are in complete control of how long you want to write: you are the one who sets the timer for one minute, five minutes, or ten minutes. In five minutes, most people will write half to two-thirds of a page. Ten minutes of rush writing produces a page or more. So if you rush-write a journal and spend only five minutes a day on it for a year, you will have a book more than two hundred pages in length. A book about you.

The advantage of writing fast, of writing your first thoughts, is that it allows you to record your thoughts before you can censor them—before you can say, "Oh, what a stupid beginning," or, "This doesn't make any sense," or, "I'm spelling this wrong." It separates the writer in you from the critic in you. Our critics encourage the myth that writing is a high and mighty thing, and unless we can do it like Virginia Woolf or Erma Bombeck, we shouldn't do it at all. I happen to think if you can talk, you can write.

Certainly you can write about your own life, which is an inexhaustible subject, and no one knows more about that subject than you. Unlike essays or critical writing, journal writing enables you to write authoritatively, without proof, evidence or footnotes. Your life is the proof. No one can argue with your experience, with your unique view of the world. It's the critic in us who tells us we can't write.

One last fear of journal writers that I have not mentioned is the fear that someone in the present will read the journal. I know a woman in Minnesota who keeps a big Yale lock on her journal so that her mother, whom she lives with, won't be able to read it. Can you think of anything more inviting than a Yale lock to make you want to read someone's journal? What exotic, sinful, secret life could she be hiding between those covers? If this is something you worry about, then use an unimportant looking spiral notebook (with Bat Man stickers on it) that no one will think to pick up.

All of this raises the question, how comfortable are we with our imperfections, our humanness, our vulnerabilities, our silliness, our pomposity? Can we live with the fact that when it's all written down, we aren't Toni Morrison or Margaret Mead or Anne Morrow Lindbergh or Joseph Smith? It's a great disappointment when we don't look better on paper. When you rush-write, you decide to be imperfect. Who can write beautifully in a five-minute, timed writing? Who can be eloquent writing as fast as she can? Count on being imperfect. It will make the writing much easier and will be a relief to your posterity.

There are many varieties of journal writing. And even though there is no "right way" to keep a journal, it's fun to know about the different techniques that journal writers use to express themselves. The more of these you know and use, the less likely you are to become bored with your own writing. The modes of expression I discuss here come from Tristine Rainer, *The New Diary* (Los Angeles: J.P. Tarcher, 1978). She also discusses — although I do not — guided imagery, altered points of view, portraits, maps of consciousness, and dialogues.

Perhaps the most common and familiar form of expression in journals is description, where we simply describe our day: "I got up, fixed the kids breakfast, etc." Descriptive writing satisfies the urge to reproduce reality as it is, better than it is, or worse than it is (Rainer, 56). Here is an example from 1983 when my son Samuel was two:

> While I was making my bed, Samuel played with the beads Ruth Anne brought him last weekend. A whole bag of them. He loaded them into a little dump truck and "drove" them along the seamline of the carpet in the closet doorway.
> "Don't eat any of them," I said. "They're not candy."
> "They're not candy," he repeated.
> I pulled the bedding toward the top of the bed and tapped the switch to the electric blanket with my slippered toe until the orange light went off.
> "Ow ow ow," Samuel howled from behind the closet door. It was a serious call for help.
> "What is it?" I asked, stumbling from behind the bed and hovering over him.
> "I have diamonds in my nose."
> "What?"
> "I have diamonds in my nose."
> A white bead gleamed from one of his nostrils. A second one was lodged so far back in the other nostril that I couldn't see it until he tilted his head back.
> "I'll get it out," I said, and began to laugh. I couldn't help it. He yelled louder at my lack of sympathy. He is my fourth son, but the first to stuff things into his nose. I

used a paper clip to pry the one bead loose and then shut
off the free nostril with my finger and told him to blow.
Out came the bead.

"Don't eat the beads and don't put them up your nose,"
I warned him.

"I won't."

Don't put them in your ears or any other holes in your
body, for that matter. Don't feed them to the dog. Don't
pour them into the piano or the typewriter. Don't press
them into white bread. Don't.

Besides describing your day, try describing yourself as you
are right now. It's a good idea to do this at least once a decade.
Here's mine from several years ago:

I am forty years old. I weigh 135 pounds and am 5
feet, 9 inches tall. Every year I watch the Miss Universe
contest. I am the right height for that contest. I watch it
to see how close I am to the weight. The last time I was
close to the weight was 1967. I am now ten pounds away
from being Miss Universe. One of my front teeth is graying
and a molar is chipped from eating a pretzel. It doesn't
hurt, so I put off getting it fixed.

My husband is a German professor at a large midwestern
university. I always thought I was like Jo March of Little
Women, who wrote stories in her attic and married a
German professor. I felt privileged, as a matter of fact,
because, after all, there aren't enough German professors
to go around for all the girls who read Little Women and
thought themselves to be like Jo in every aspect. I find,

now that I am 40, that not all of us wanted German professors in the first place. I did, though.

I was always mildly depressed during the long Minnesota winters. Here is a description from that period of my life:

It's mid-February and thawing. A steady drip of water falls from the roof onto the deck. The backyard is the color of cement. Jonathan has hung a bird feeder in the maple tree. It is made out of a plastic milk carton with a yellow pencil poked into it for a perch. I sat on the sofa in my bathrobe, sipped hot chocolate, and watched a squirrel swat at the bird feeder. The squirrel made me happy. So I walked into the kitchen and removed the "Tips for Coping with Depression" from the refrigerator door, stuck there a month before with two yellow arrow magnets. I never followed any of the suggestions. The first one said, "Get up and do something." I never did.

One of my students, Kristine Hansen Widtfeldt, describes scenes from her childhood in her journal. This is a good idea, because she's killing two birds with one stone: she's keeping a journal and also writing the story of her life. Genealogy on five minutes a day!

Tammy Myers is my best friend and has been since the third grade. We have decided that this is a long time and that we need to consummate our relationship by becoming blood sisters. We are in her bathroom, and I'm sitting on the toilet, which has a Donald Duck seat cover. I'm staring at a plaque under the mirror which says, "We aim to please. You aim too, please." Tammy says her mother put it there for her brothers.

Tammy and I are exasperated. "You know," Tammy mumbles, "I never thought making yourself bleed would be so hard." A sewing needle, a steak knife, and a monogrammed letter opener are arranged in a careful row on the formica countertop. We had tried them all without even a scratch.

"Wait—I think Gordon has a switchblade in his dresser—"

I jerk up off the toilet. "I'm not using a switchblade."

"But—"

"I don't care," I say stubbornly. "I'm not cutting myself with a switchblade."

Tammy asks me if I want to forget the whole thing, and I tell her I don't, which is the truth. We have been best friends since the third grade, after all. Tammy suddenly hits on an alternative: "Wait. I know what would be even better than blood sisters—" Her look tells me to resume my seat on the Donald Duck toilet cover, which I do. "We could be SPIT sisters." Her eyebrows are raised and she is waiting.

"Gross," I say, disgusted.

"Exactly. We'll be the only two spit sisters at Lincoln Middle School." I guess she senses my usual reticence, so she adds, "You won't have to bleed . . . come on, it'll be cool."

As usual, my reticence gives way to Tammy's determination, and she plucks two Dixie cups from the blue dispenser on the wall. She tells me to spit into it until it is *full to the brim. I have not brushed my teeth since lunch, and the Cheetos I ate return as tiny orange specks in my saliva.*

When the cups are full, we trade.

I look at my charge with anxiety and nausea. Tammy's spit is bubblier than mine, but the familiar Cheeto-specks hang like pineapple suspended in Jello. Tammy tells me to pretend it's just Coke, or to concentrate on something else. "We aim to please. You aim too, please."

Together we count to three, plug our noses, and swallow.

The whole mass goes down as a slimy unit, like a raw egg or a live garden slug. I shudder massively and look up at Tammy, who is red-faced and triumphant.

She smiles broadly and manages, "Congratulations, sis —" before she convulses and throws up in the sink.

Another student describes one of her first memories:

My earliest memory was thinking that my dad was Mr. Rogers. Every night, I'd watch my favorite show, Mr. Rogers, and run up to the TV and yell, "Daddy! Daddy!" I listened to all the information Mr. Rogers had for me. When the show was over, my dad would usually come home. It seemed so logical to me then and I can distinctly remember nights when the moment the show was over, I would hear the key in the door and my dad would walk in. It was probably the happiest time of my life.

Another form of expression in journal writing is called cathartic writing. That is writing done under intense emotion (Rainer, 53). Often the physical writing itself takes on the emotion of the writer. For example, when I'm angry, I press my pen so hard on the page that it makes grooves into several pages of the journal. I know a young teenager who writes when she's in love and dots her "i"s with hearts. Cathartic writing is often punctuated with frequent exclamation points.

Sophie Tolstoy, the wife of the great Russian novelist, Leo Tolstoy, wrote a cathartic diary in which she sounds mostly angry:

> I am nothing but a miserable crushed worm, whom no one wants, whom no one loves, a useless creature with morning sickness, and a big belly, two rotten teeth, and a bad temper, a battered sense of dignity, and a love which nobody wants and which nearly drives me insane. ("Sophie Tolstoy [1844–1919]," Revelations: Diaries of Women, ed. Mary Jane Moffat and Charlotte Painter [New York: Vintage, 1975], 144)

Her diary reads on and on like this, and then suddenly, the reader comes upon one completely different entry:

> It makes me laugh to read over this diary. It's so full of contradictions, and one would think I was such an unhappy woman. Yet is there a happier woman than I? It would be hard to find a happier or more friendly marriage than ours. Sometimes, when I am alone in the room, I just laugh with joy, and making the sign of the cross, say to myself, "May God let this last many, many years." ("Tolstoy," 144)

Cathartic writing isn't very pretty (Rainer, 53). Some people feel like they are exposing an ugly side of themselves and avoid it altogether. But when it is juxtaposed with other, more tempered kinds of journal writings, the overall effect is a journal written by a well-rounded individual. Here is an example of cathartic writing from one of my students:

> *I am so mad I could just scream!!!!!! I hate my bank so much!!!!!!!!! I can't believe that they won't let me deposit money into my checking account here in Utah. I understand my account is based in Arizona. But let's be serious about this. My bank is First Interstate. A big nationwide bank. On their commercials they advertise their nationwide service, but if you try to do anything over state lines it is completely stupid. I am so dang mad!! #$*(&&(#! ##$% %% & & &**& *(*&*&)(*& Now I have bounced a check. That is just great for my credit. Tomorrow morning they're going to be hearing from me in person. Face to face. They're going to know just how upset I really am. ARRGH!!*

Here is an example from my own journal, written Saturday, January 23, 1982:

> *I'm in such a foul mood. We got up too late and cleaned the house, which looked like it belonged to poor white trash. Dog doo doos all over the living room. I kicked the dog in sheer exasperation and yelled wild threats to everyone within hearing range such as, "I'm going to flush this dog down the toilet!" Blah, blah, blah. Jonathan said that if I did that, he would sell my new red jacket. I said that if he did that, I would stuff him in a box and send him back to Boston, general delivery. It wasn't a safe place here today.*

A kind of writing closely related to cathartic writing is called free writing. It is useful when you feel like you should be writing in your diary, but you can't think of a thing to write about. Simply clear your mind of everything, set the timer, and write down whatever comes into your head. Students like this kind of writing a lot. Here is a sample of a student's free writing:

> It's 8:14. Do you know where your children are? Do you know where your parents are? Do you know where the presidential candidates are? Do you know who the presidential candidates are? Do you care? Does it matter? Does Rodney Dangerfield deserve any respect? Is Elvis really dead? Does it matter? What is your major? Does it matter? Is there such a thing as antimatter? Why does Captain Kirk always get the girl? Did Mr. Spock ever make out in the back of the space station as a young spockling? Does it matter?
>
> It's 8:17. Does it matter?

Another kind of journal writing is reflective writing, where you pull back to assess and evaluate your own life (Rainer, 68).

Florida Scott Maxwell, in her wonderful diary called A Measure of My Days, reflects on what it is like to be old. She was eighty-two when she wrote this:

> Age puzzles me. I thought it was a quiet time. My seventies were interesting and fairly serene, but my eighties are passionate. I grow more intense as I age. To my own surprise, I burst out with hot conviction. Only a few years

ago I enjoyed my tranquillity, now I am so disturbed by
the outer world and by human quality in general, that I
want to put things right as though I still owed a debt to
life. I must calm down. I am far too frail to indulge in
moral fervour. ("Florida Scott Maxwell," Revelations,
362)

And this is one of my favorites:

No matter how old a mother is, she watches her middle-
aged children for signs of improvement. ("Maxwell," 362)

Descriptive, cathartic, reflective, and even free writing are
fairly typical of inexperienced journal writers, but there are
other techniques not used as frequently that are a whole lot
of fun. My favorite is list making. A list of your fears, your
hopes, the contents of your purse can often say as much or
more about your life than three pages of prose. If you want to
spend only one or two minutes writing in your journal instead
of the lengthy five minutes, then write a list. Here is a list of
possible lists:

1. Write a list of everyone you have ever loved.
2. Write a list of all the teachers you ever had.
3. Write a list of your fears.
4. Write a list of pleasures you enjoyed during the day.
5. Write a list of what is in your refrigerator before you
go shopping and then write another list after you go shopping.
6. Write a list that begins, "How my life would be different
if I had gone to college," or, "How my life would be different
if I had not joined the Church," or, "How my life would be
different if I hadn't married Tom," or, "How I would spend

my money if I won the Publisher's Clearing House sweep-stakes."

7. Write a list of everything you've done since the last time you wrote in your journal.

When I was thirty, I wrote a list called "On being realistic at age thirty." Some of the items:

> Being realistic at age thirty means realizing that you will never hobnob it with the Burtons, or the Rockefellers, with Walter Cronkite or Alice Roosevelt Longworth, with Kurt Vonnegut, Jr., or Lillian Hellman, and who cares anyway.
>
> Being realistic at age thirty means realizing that you do not have that well preserved look.
>
> Being realistic at age thirty is realizing that you whine.
>
> Being realistic at age thirty means realizing that your husband doesn't want to be an apostle.

List everything you have in your wallet today. It will be different from what you have in there next week or next year. Here is a list of what was in my wallet yesterday:

> 3 cents
> a receipt from Le Boulangerie pastry shop on the corner of California and Hyde in San Francisco — to remember the delightful breakfasts we had each morning during our vacation last Christmas
> a book of postage stamps
> a business card from the Ling Ling Panda restaurant on Center Street in Provo
> a little piece of paper with my parents' address in Switzerland

a Conoco card
a Weinstock's card
a Deseret Healthcare card
a BYU ID card
a Sears credit card
a Citibank Visa card.
a Provo Library card
my driver's license
a check guarantee card
a Kinko's discount card

That's my life in my wallet. Here is a list one of my students wrote. It is called "Weird things I can do with my body":

I can . . .
1. *Move my scalp back and forth*
2. *Make my eyes twitch*
3. *Move my ears up and down*
4. *Flair my nostrils*
5. *Suck my cheeks together until they touch*
6. *Make bird sounds*
7. *Bend my fingers way back*
8. *Crack my left thumb continuously*
9. *Protrude my stomach*
10. *Cross the two middle toes on my right foot*

Another list from one of my students: "Things I would have done differently if I were doing my wedding over":

1. *I would have bought the dress I really loved instead of buying a cheaper one.*

2. I would have spent the evening before my wedding with David rather than fixing my dress.

3. I wouldn't have stood in a receiving line for three hours.

4. I would have made people be quiet so I could hear the quartet.

5. I would have danced a waltz with David.

6. I would have left the reception earlier.

7. I would have taken a longer honeymoon.

Here is Kevin Pugh's list of everything he's caught while fishing:

Fish: rainbow trout, brook trout, brown trout, cutthroat trout, grayling, silver salmon, sock-eye salmon, dog salmon, hook-jawed salmon, big salmon, red salmon, dead salmon (believe it or not I caught a 100% dead salmon), white fish, chubs, carp, blue gil, perch, albino fish, great big fish, including one 12-pound rainbow, little tiny fish — I think three inches is the smallest, hybrid rainbow trout, planter fish, native fish.

Things other than fish: my neck, my hand, my foot, my finger, my leg, my waders, my hat, my shirt, my sunglasses (thank goodness I had them on), my fly rod, my friend, my dad, my guide, my boat, my float tube, trees, bushes, rocks, moss, sticks, flowers, a bat almost, and even the car door.

In reply to Betty Tobler's friend who could not make a list of "good things" about Orem, Utah, I made this list (I had lived away from Utah for twenty years):

1. *Apple and cherry trees in blossom.*
2. *The mountain view out of all the east windows.*
3. *Never having to explain your Mormonness.*
4. *The University Mall.*
5. *A new interest in the Cape Cod house, which is a classic and beautiful design.*
6. *A short drive to Provo Canyon. I saw a pond with white geese on it and seven skunks scurrying around it.*
7. *A church on every corner.*
8. *Pinenuts.*
9. *The mild winter season.*
10. *The sky is bluer here.*

My sister Janie and I sat up late one night listing everyone who ever lived in Emigration Ward when we were growing up. We drew a map of our neighborhood and listed the people who had lived in each house. There was no reason for doing this, except to recall our past together, to remember.

My ultimate list is the one where I listed everything that was under my bed when I finally cleaned under there (see "Thoughts of a Grasshopper," p. 9). It not only reveals my glaring negligence in housekeeping but it also reveals the fabric of my life that year: I was teaching early morning seminary, which is why there were Exodus worksheets under the bed. My husband was having a midlife crisis, which is why there were notes about alternative ways of making a living. The list reveals that we like to eat in bed, read in bed, write in bed. The list also reveals that we must have had a bed the size of New Jersey. I wish my Dutch grandmothers had made just a few lists.

People often daydream in their journals, but I like to write my night dreams as well. Dreams have an odd quality that combines realism and fantasy, present life with past life, anxieties and hopes. My friend Bonnie Fisher is a poet who lives in Minneapolis. For a period of time she woke herself up in the middle of the night so she could record her dreams. She found that she had a series of pea-soup dreams:

Last night I dreamed my mother was making pea soup.
I sat at her table with an empty bowl.
She didn't seem to see me and gave all the soup to the cat.

I dream I am making pea soup because Natalie is coming.
I set the steaming kettle in the sink while I answer the phone.
It is my mother calling long distance. Static on the line, I can't
tell what she wants. Water is running into the dishpan, it
overflows, soapy and tepid into the soup kettle. My soup
is ruined now and Natalie will not come.

In my dream I ladle out soup into a bowl for my daughter,
Catherine. Her hair, long and snarled, hangs over her
hopeful eyes. I have no dreams for her. I don't know how
to love her. I know there are snakes in this soup I have
made, and I ladle carefully trying not to give her any.

I dream my sister Peggy is coming to see me, and I think I
should make her soup and clean up my house. But I don't.
When she comes, things will be just like this, and I will be as
I am, and we will rummage together through the refrigerator
if we get hungry.

The first time I read these "pea soup dreams," I asked Bonnie what she thought they meant. She said she didn't know but her mother often made pea soup for her when she was a child and it made her feel nurtured and secure.

Here is an anxiety dream (most of my dreams are anxiety dreams) that I recorded when I was in graduate school at the University of Minnesota:

> I go back and forth to the university on wooden stilts. I go home via Oak Street and walk very fast down the entrance ramp to Highway 94. I can keep up with the cars on my stilts. Large faces without bodies line the south side of the highway. They are there to cheer for me because I am so fast on my stilts. Suddenly I am back again on the entrance ramp, but when I look down I find I'm on different stilts and up about three stories from the cars below. I am moving too fast onto the highway and feel out of control with these longer stilts. The principle is the same, I think, but the height panics me. I turn to call to Tom way below me. "These stilts are too high," I shout. He can't hear me. "How will I get down?" I can only imagine falling on my face on the asphalt.

The following dream seemed so real that I was relieved upon waking to find that I really was not a thief:

> Charles and I are pulling shoe boxes of papers down from a closet shelf. We browse through the papers. They are names of people who have contributed money to Salt Lake's Hansen Planetarium. As we look them over, we both realize that I have stolen $600 from the planetarium

funds. I can hardly believe I have done such a thing, but
Charles insists it is true. I try to remember if I ever did
volunteeer work for the planetarium. I cannot remember,
but I have a vague dread that I have repressed my work
for them, so I would not have to face the fact that I stole
$600 from them. Then I recall that Brooks Briggs and
Brady Udall, two students from my creative writing class,
had given me a huge brown envelope of papers months
before, asking me to do some volunteer work for the planetarium. I guess it was then I stole the money. I feel
mortified. Then I am standing in the front foyer of the
planetarium. The police have come to arrest me for stealing
$600. One detective goes to put the handcuffs on me and
I shrink back and say, "You don't have to do that. I won't
run away." He says, "I'm sorry, ma'am. It's policy."
He handcuffs my hands behind my back. Several policemen
and detectives and I walk down the steps of the planetarium
toward a waiting squad car. B. is standing on the sidewalk
wearing an eight-hundred-dollar suit. At first when I see
that he is witnessing this whole awful ordeal, I am ashamed,
but as I walk past him, I nod at him and think, "So what?"

One of my favorite dreams belongs to my student Kristine
Hansen Widtfeldt, who was not married when she wrote this:

I am pregnant when I wake up this morning, although
I do not notice it until I am in the shower, and I drop the
soap and cannot pick it up. My stomach is too big. "Oh,"
I think, "I am pregnant. I guess I'll have to wear my
elastic-waisted jeans skirt to campus."
When I get out of the shower, my roommates all com-

ment, "Hey, Kristine, you're pregnant." I tell them yes. In class, my professors notice — "You are pregnant." Yes, I tell them, and they tell me that is nice.

After classes, I decide to go shopping for maternity clothes, as I can't wear this jeans skirt for the rest of my pregnancy. I walk into K-Mart and ask the obese woman behind the service desk where to find maternity clothes. She tells me I am pregnant, and I tell her yes, that I know. She asks who the father is, and I suddenly realize I have no idea. "You can't try on maternity clothes without knowing who the father is," she tells me. She offers to help. She twists around this huge metal microphone which is attached to the service desk: "Attention, K-Mart Shoppers," the obese clerk says, "whoever is the father of Kristine's child, will you please come up to the service desk?" Hoards of balding men, with age spots on their foreheads and wearing plaid flannel shirts, start emerging from the aisles. They walk like zombies, and I am scared. I run past them into the maternity department, which is by the layaway department. There is a dressing room there and I run in and close the door. The dressing room is a tiny pressboard cubicle, and I am now too big even to turn around inside it. I am afraid, and I stay in the dressing room until the store is closed.

The idea painlessly comes to me that the baby wants to be born — now, and here in the K-Mart dressing room. "Hey," I yell, "somebody let me out. I'm having a baby." But no one is in the store, and I have the baby alone. She is a girl and I will call her Corolla.

The following is my husband's favorite of all my dreams. Obviously, he has some not very latent hostilities:

My husband left me for another woman. She was a short, dowdy person with a chipped front tooth. I begged him to stay, but he couldn't hear me. He invited the four boys to the wedding ceremony. I drove them to the church. They left me alone in the car. I got out and stood under a leafless oak tree and tapped my foot to the wedding march.

It was important that the marriage not be consummated. I followed my husband and his bride to the honeymoon cottage. When the lights went out, I began running my fingernails over the screen door and then went around to each screened window. I circled the house, scratching screens until I heard his beloved say, "I can't—not with that awful noise. Make her go away."

"I'll call the police," said my husband. I heard the sirens but could not stop scratching the screens with my fingernails. The police hauled me away. They thought I was crazy.

It's entertaining to muse about what dreams might mean, but it certainly is not necessary. For me, it is interesting to know that my subconscious is at work while I'm sleeping. A journal that records dreams reveals wishes, anxieties, warnings, and questions, sometimes all side by side with each other. They reveal a kind of vague, personal truth. I enjoy rereading them.

A journal-writing mode that I picked up quite naturally as a teenager is writing unsent letters. The first complete journal I began at age fifteen was written in letter form to "Mimi." I got the name from combining *me* plus *me*, and then changing the spelling. It must have been important, because I painstakingly explain all of this in the first few pages. Since then, my unsent letters have taken a more cathartic turn. I use them to yell at people I would not yell at in person. I yell with my pen. What is useful about this is that often my anger dissipates after these written shoutings. None of them is readable. They read very much like one of my student's unsent letters that begins, *"Dear Scott, What a pig you are!"* Another student wrote this one:

> *Wayne, you are a jerk, and a very big one at that. I don't know what makes you think that I was interested in you and your candy-apple red Porsche with the quadraphonic Blaupunkt stereo. It does not impress me and neither do you. I've tried very nicely telling you this before, but your ego will just not let your brain hear it.*
>
> *Your car is dumb, Wayne. You are dumb. Those three dozen green and blue carnations gave me hayfever, and the color rubbed off on my hands as I threw them away. Your white John Travolta suit is dumb. Your five gold chains that you insisted on wearing constantly are tacky, and NO I will not go to Las Vegas with you. I don't know what else to say except no, no, no.*
>
> *Have a decent life.*

Unsent letters need not necessarily be angry ones. I have had students write letters to a grandparent who has died:

> *Dear Grandma Wheaton, I feel so bad that I never got to meet you. I was only three when you died, and hard as I try to remember anything at all about you, I can't. Mom*

still talks about you all the time. She says you were the
best whistler she ever heard. She wishes she had a recording
of you whistling "White Wings." I wish it too.

I have had students who wrote to deceased authors to tell
them how much they enjoyed their work:

Dear Ralph Waldo Emerson, Do you know how famous
you still are? You made it into the Norton Anthology of
American Literature!

My son Charles likes to draw pictures using stylized figures
that often are dancing or running through meadows. In his
journal, he wrote a letter to one of these male figures:

Who are you? And what makes you so free? I created
you, so why don't I feel as free as you? You slide down
rainbows. You run above the tree tops; you dance on silver-
lined clouds. You run, skate, dance, and fly. What did I
give you that makes you special and makes me want to be
like you instead of who I really am? Who am I really?
Why did I create you if you just make me envious of your
life? Why is it that you, as a two-dimensional character,
have more freedom than I do as a three-dimensional person?
How can you be cheerful and free while I feel oppressed
by reality? I often think that we'd all be better off being
like you!

My favorite unsent letter was written by my neighbor,
Dessie Thomas, when she was eighty-four years old. She was
asked by a Relief Society teacher to write a letter to her
husband, who had passed away five years before. Dessie was

reluctant, but when she tried it, she found that she enjoyed
the task. I know that we who heard her read it in Relief
Society were profoundly moved by it:

> *Earth, June 22, 1986*
> *My dearly beloved Edwin,*
> *Where are you, and how are you? You seem so far*
> *away and the daily letters you used to write when away*
> *from home fail to come now. I'm so grateful for any*
> *communication from you. The dream I had of you recently*
> *was so dear to me. Come again. I need you.*
>
> *The boys and their wives are very kind and thoughtful*
> *of me, but they have their own heavy family, professional,*
> *and church responsibilities. I do not wish to impose unduly.*
> *What I need is my own dear "fix-it-man" who always*
> *kept everything in repair. You spoiled me for life alone.*
>
> *How I long to have your strong comforting arms around*
> *me and have all my cares and worries melt away in your*
> *embrace. You were always magic in my life. I'm afraid I*
> *failed to tell you that often enough. I hope a heavenly*
> *messenger will deliver my thoughts of gratitude to you.*
>
> *I pray for you in your work each day. I want to give*
> *you the same loyal support I did in your work here. I'm*
> *eager to hear of all the wonderful things you are doing*
> *there.*
>
> *I have just finished reading the love letters of William*
> *and Mary Wordsworth. They were sweet, but lacked the*
> *depth of our letters to each other. I'm sure it is the Gospel*
> *that makes the difference. You know, Edwin, I have been*
> *sorting our letters by dates in an effort to tell our story*

through letters. This is a project I have wanted to complete
ever since you went away. Last week I read over three
hundred — the letters we wrote during our romancing days.
They were so sweet and tender — full of hope and trust for
our future. Somehow, I don't want to share them with
anyone. I would like to bring them with me when I come.
We could laugh and cry as we read them together the first
week of our reunion. One dream expressed over and over
again was the hope that we would spare at least one hour
for each other daily in our married life.

It was wonderful being so completely yours, Edwin. We
worried about being so far away from our families, but it
made our relationship even closer. After you went away,
I realized that you were not only my devoted husband, but
had become my mother, my father, my brother, my sister,
my friend — my everything.

Now you are gone. You always went on ahead with
every new job assignment and left me to sell or rent our
home, get the children through school, etc., before I followed. Each time we would say, "We will never do this
again. Life is too short to be apart." And now you made
this major move without me. Why couldn't we have taken
each other by the hand and walked out into space together?
I guess that way would be too easy for growth.

When we were studying the Psalms in Sunday School,
I wrote this psalm in your memory:

My soul longeth for my husband.
Oh, give me strength and peace, dear Lord.
I know thy goodness and mercy. Thou hast been with me
    through many troubles.

My faith in Thee hath grown through tribulations.
I have tested Thy love for me through answered prayers.
O praise Thy name, my anchor and hope — my strength and
*   my salvation.*
In this special time of need, make me worthy of the help I
*   seek,*
Thy sweet companionship, comfort, and strength through
*   Thee. Amen.*

I am waiting for your call to join you.
*   Your loving wife,*
*   Dessie*

Even though this is an unsent letter, I like to think he got the message.

Writing a journal is a way of making a mark in the world — our own personal mark. The kinds of exercises I have offered here are merely a sampling of the many ways of making that mark. There are others: writing dialogues, writing portraits about people we know well, writing rhymed verse. It doesn't all have to be writing, either. It can be drawing pictures or maps of houses we've lived in, neighborhoods, schools. It can be cutting and pasting. It can be tracing our right hand into the front cover as I did when I was fifteen, or leaving an imprint of our lips on the back cover.

To read old journals is to see both the sadness and humor of our lives. Possibly we write journals for our posterity — I think so less and less. In any case, if anyone down the line is remotely interested in my life, I'd rather have them read it from my voice than from the voice of a grandson or granddaughter who knew me only as an old lady. I will write it myself. It takes only five minutes a day.

A Christmas Romance

PROLOGUE

This is one of those romance novels. You know, the disgusting kind with kisses that last three paragraphs and make you want to put your finger down your throat to induce longrange vomiting. It is one of those books where the hero has a masculine sounding name that ends in an unvoiced velar plosive like *Chuck* (although that is not my hero's name), and he has sinewy muscles and makes gutteral groanings whenever his beloved is near. In romance novels, the heroine has a feminine-sounding name made up of liquid consonants like *Fleur* and has full, sensuous lips — yearning lips. I think the word "yearning" will appear at least a thousand times in this book. The heroine also has long, silky legs and is a virgin.

The reason I know about romance novels at all is because my best friend, Ashley, was addicted to them last year, our junior year. I don't think addicted is too strong a word here. She received eight romances in the mail every month through some kind of romance book club, and she read them all in a couple of days and insisted I read them too. She'd buy more in used book stores for a dime apiece and then trade them with other girls like comic books. The trouble with romance novels, I soon discovered, is that they make you feel bad about your life, especially if there is no Chuck in it, and especially if you don't have long silky legs and your name ends in an unvoiced dental plosive like mine does (Kate), and very especially if you think you're going to be a virgin for the rest of your life. Mostly, though, romance novels are sappy in the extreme. They read like junior-high-school daydreams. I've never read one that I could really believe. None of them sounds like real life. And I want real life. Even in novels, I want real life.

So what do you do if you have lived a real romance, and it happened at Christmas, and the guy has a masculine-sounding name, Richard, and it ends up that he loves you as much as you love him? I know what I want to do. I want to write a romance novel about it. I want it to end with "they lived happily ever after." And indeed we have.

Sort of. This all happened last December, and it is now the middle of February, so we have lived happily ever after for six weeks. But how many people do you know who are exhilaratingly happy for six weeks? I know it's a record for me.

I want to gloat and bask in this lovely feeling of being in love. And if I do not have long, silky legs, long, blonde locks, I do have sensuous, full lips; and if I have not written three-paragraph kisses, I have kissed them.

I'm giving this my best shot. I've got *The Romance Writer's Phrase Book* right next to the word processor in case I am at a loss for words, as they say. If you are jaded about romance or have PMS or are on the down side of manic-depression and can't stand to read about other people's happiness, then get real. This book is not for you.

CHAPTER ONE OF A ROMANCE NOVEL is the chapter where the heroine is described and where she first meets the hero. This is no different. It happened a few days before Christmas. My mother asked me to walk down to Sims Market after dinner and get some cinnamon sticks. She has this hot drink she makes around Christmas called Russian tea — it's filled with cinnamon and cloves and sugar and orange and lemon and stuff, and we guzzle it all through the holidays. It's part of our family tradition, this drink. Anyway, she was out of cinnamon sticks. Would I go to Sims?

It was a dark and stormy night.

That is the honest-to-gosh truth. I live in Saint Paul, Minnesota, and it was snowing hard — large flakes the size of cotton balls — and it thundered and flashed lightning off in the distance. If you don't believe thunder and lightning can accompany snow, then obviously you haven't lived in Minnesota, the weather state.

I covered my *six-foot, lithe* frame in thermal underwear, ski pants, a turtleneck sweater, a down parka with the hood up, mittens with reindeer heads knitted into the tops, and million-dollar snow boots, which my father calls "the fruit boots." I'm not going to apologize for being too tall. I know heroines should be petite, but this is *my* novel, and I'm not going to pretend to be shorter than I am. I am six feet in my stocking feet. I do have very long legs and nice knee caps, but I don't know if they're particularly silky. In fact, sometimes in winter, when I'm totally covered in clothes all the time, I just skip shaving my legs and see how long the hairs can get. A kind of contest with myself. If I want silky legs, I can get them by rubbing Chanel body lotion all over them.

Anyway, the minute I began walking down Folwell Street, I felt glad to be alive. Even before the hero entered, I was pretty happy with my life. I'm not the sulking type. My father, the linguistics professor, had been playing one of *The Brandenburg Concertos* when I left the house, and I felt as if the flute music was trapped inside of me and that if I opened my mouth, it would trill out into the night air. I caught snowflakes on my tongue the way I used to do when I was ten. The night felt magical. There must have been some foreshadowing in the air.

It's only about six blocks to Sims Market, and pretty soon I was standing in front of the spices, but I couldn't find the cinnamon sticks. I knew they were arranged in alphabetical order, but my eyes (which *The Romance Writer's Phrase Book* would describe as "amethyst") skipped from basil to fennel to thyme and back again. There were distractions: the canned music, for one thing. I stood directly under a speaker blaring an orchestral rendition of "Sleigh Bells" and found myself trying to fill in the words, "Just hear those sleigh bells jingling, ring ting tingling . . . " Then what? "It's lovely weather — something, something — together with you." Basil, fennel, thyme.

The other distraction was Ashley, my best friend, who taught me all there was to know about the romance novel last year, and her boyfriend, Kirk, at the checkout counter making much ado about the dry mistletoe forlornly hung over each checkout aisle. They held the blue plastic shopping basket between them, but Kirk leaned over it, threatening to kiss Ashley in front of clerks and customers alike. Finally he bit her ear, and Ashley's laughter pealed above the canned "Sleigh

Bells." When heads turned, Ashley muffled her mouth as if she had committed a grand social *faux pas*. Kirk took her hand and put it in the pocket of his parka with his own after they set the filled shopping basket on the counter.

The truth is that Ashley is always trying to live her life as if she were the heroine of a romance novel. It never works though. She rarely lives happily ever after, even for six weeks. But at Christmastime, she and Kirk were hot for each other.

I tried to concentrate on the spices. Allspice, sweet basil, ground cinnamon—

"Kate!" Ashley flounced down the aisle in front of Kirk, who carried the brown sack of groceries. "I didn't know you were in the store!" Her voice is all dramatic and different when she's with Kirk. I never want to sound different from myself around any guy.

"Oh, hi, you guys!" I nod at Kirk. "Mother needed some cinnamon sticks and I wanted a walk in the snow, so—"

"Isn't it romantic out there tonight? Kirk and I are going to make Christmas cookies together." Ashley slipped her arm through Kirk's.

"*You're* going to make them. *I'm* going to eat them." Kirk wagged his tongue at Ashley.

"No, you're going to help measure and mix too, and—" Ashley bumped hips with him, "you're going to wear an apron."

"No way." Kirk pretended to back off, but Ashley held on to him. "You'll love cooking. It's a *sensuous* activity."

The way Ashley said "sensuous" with an exaggerated pout of the lips directed at Kirk made me think that the conversation was about more than just baking cookies. There was romance-novel stuff smouldering below the surface of cookie-dough chat. "Sounds like fun," I said.

"We'd better go," Ashley said. "My parents won't be gone all night."

"Unfortunately," Kirk muttered.

Ashley laughed and patted his chest. "Oh, you," she said.

Watching Ashley and Kirk was as depressing as reading a romance novel. I felt like they were performing for my benefit. "Save a cookie for me," I said.

"Of course, *mon ami*," Ashley said.

Give it a rest, Ashley. That's what I wanted to say.

She turned Kirk around with a grand sweep of her arm. She was a different person entirely around Kirk. A looney tune.

"See you later," Kirk said, looking back.

He didn't gaze longingly into my amethyst eyes, so he obviously is not the hero in this novel.

At the end of the aisle Ashley shouted back, "Isn't Christmas wonderful?"

What she really meant was, isn't Christmas wonderful when you're going with someone whose name ends in an unvoiced velar plosive like Kirk.

I forced a laugh for her and waved good-bye. "Have fun, Ash," I called. Like I said, I was happy all the way to Sims Market, but now I felt let down a little. I actually sighed. I was jealous of Ashley and Kirk. A lot jealous, but I did not, as *The Romance Writer's Phrase Book* says, "flounder in an agonizing maelstrom." I'm too buoyant for that. I just admitted I was a little jealous, and at the same time I did this, I realized there weren't any cinnamon sticks on the shelf.

"Mr. Sims." I turned when I smelled the cigarette smoke.

Mr. Sims is the last chain smoker in Minnesota and completely ignores the clean-air act. "It's my store," he says when customers complain. He's known around the neighborhood as "that jerk."

"Do you have any cinnamon sticks in the back? There's none on the shelf."

"If it's not on the shelf, I don't have any," he said, bending over a broken sack of sugar.

I tried not to stare at his thick moustache when he looked up. It always had gunk in it.

"Won't have any until next week." Ashes fell from his cigarette into the open sugar bag.

"But that's after Christmas." The only time my mother used cinnamon sticks was for the Russian tea at Christmas.

"So?" Mr. Sims lifted the broken sugar bag and blew smoke into my face.

I waved the smoke away. "So nothing." I pulled the cigarette from his lips and stuffed it lit-end first into the sugar. "Smoking will kill you," I said and walked off, feeling pretty powerful.

"What business is that of yours?" he called after me.

"Merry Christmas, Mr. Sims," I said.

He said something I couldn't hear. Probably bah humbug. I didn't care. I knew Mr. Sims would become a minor, flat character in my novel.

Outside, it was still a dark and stormy night: it snowed steadily. I pulled the hood of my parka up and tied it securely under my chin. Most of the stores in "the Park," which is what the one commercial street in this old suburb of Saint

Paul is called, were still open. Pine bows, red ribbons, and tiny lights decorated the store fronts. That Christmas stuff made me feel festive, and I considered stopping at Bridgeman's for hot chocolate with that synthetic whipped cream on top, but then I saw Ashley and Kirk at the end of the block. Not wanting to run into them a second time, I crossed with the light and headed home. I can only stand so much hormonal happiness in one evening, especially someone else's. I wondered if Mr. Sims had ever been in love at Christmas. Had he ever been someone's hero? There had been a Mrs. Sims years ago. Who could stand to kiss those nicotine-stained lips?

When I thought about it, climbing the long, sloping hill toward my house, happiness at Christmas was hierarchical. People in love like Ashley and Kirk were the happiest. Next came people like me, who had family and friends, and who, at least, expected to be in love at some future Christmas. Last came people like Mr. Sims — the cantankerous ones — who were never happy, and no amount of external magic, even Christmas magic, could change that.

At the top of the hill I turned the corner. I was on my street now. Through the lighted window I saw the Chamberlain twins dropping toys from their bunkbeds in their second-story bedroom. I still think of that house as the Bradshaw house, even though they moved to California four years ago. I always pass it with a kind of "upsurge of devouring yearning," as the phrase book says. But I don't think it's necessary to explain why, yet. All you need to know is that that night I passed the house, which used to be the Bradshaws' but is now the Chamberlains', with an excess of yearning. The holidays bring on those hokey feelings.

Up the street I passed the Midgely house, where Mr.
Midgely, who is younger than my father, was dying of pan-
creatic cancer. He had already lived two years longer than the
doctors said he would. It had been weeks since I had seen his
jaundiced, sunken face. There is nothing in *The Romance
Writer's Phrase Book* to help me describe that face. He used
to be the basketball coach at the high school and was also my
sophomore English teacher but had to quit this year because
of the cancer. Whenever I think of him now, I think of that
Dylan Thomas poem:

> *The force that through the green fuse drives the flower
> Drives my Green age; that blasts the roots of trees
> Is my destroyer.*

Was Mr. Midgely happy at Christmastime?
    Why this grim reflecting in a romance novel? Have I lost
control of the writing? Or is it possible that all that yearning
for the Bradshaws has turned my brain to Cheerios?
    Moving right along: the house had changed since I had
been at Sim's. More windows were lit, for one thing. Even
my bedroom light was on upstairs. Not my doing, either. I
take after my father that way, economical and practical. My
mother and Bjorn leave lights blazing all over the place, but
Bjorn was in Palo Alto, two thousand miles away with Trish
and baby Jason. Mother had been in the basement when I
left, wrapping pots of forced tulips in silver tinsel and plaid
ribbon as Christmas gifts for neighbors when I left for the
market. Weird. The house looked like a shimmering space
ship freshly landed from some exotic star. And I'm not quoting
the phrase book, either.

On the porch, brushing the snow from my collar and stomping my boots, I noticed the strange station wagon parked in the driveway. Company. Company changed a house.

Light, warm air and my brother's voice spilled through the widening crack in the front door when I opened it: "We couldn't stand another snowless Christmas this year, and when you said there was already two feet of snow on the ground, we decided to come."

"Is that you, Bjorn Bjorkman?" I yelled, pushing the front door shut with my behind. We collided between the hall and the dining room. "Boo, it's good to see you." We hugged. He still wore his parka.

"You're here!" was all I could say. I just couldn't believe it. I pulled back to see his face. His glasses were partially fogged as they always were when he came in from the cold. I pinched his arm. "It's like magic to have you here," I said.

"It took three whole days to drive here; that's not magic."

Trish appeared behind his shoulder, and I broke loose to hug my sister-in-law. "I'm so glad to see you," I said.

"Kate, you look wonderful. I like your hair that way."

"Boo. Call her Boo," Bjorn insisted. "That's her name."

"Kate fits her better than Boo, I think," Trish said.

"Thanks. I'm glad you think so. No one calls me Boo except Bjorn and his ape friends," I said.

"You mean me?" Richard Bradshaw filled the doorway.

Okay, a flourish of trumpets here. The hero has arrived. And because he was my hero long before I began writing this novel, ever since I can remember, in fact, my face grew hot. He was four years older, of course, and taller than I remembered. His eyes—I need the help of *The Romance Writer's Phrase Book* to describe those eyes:

— "unfathomable in their murky depths"?

No!

— "shades of amber and green"?

Maybe.

— "dark gray-green flecked eyes"?

I don't know. Maybe.

— "hooded like those of a hawk"?

Absolutely not! They were warm eyes. They were Richard's eyes. I wouldn't care if they were cone-shaped. Richard Bradshaw was standing in the doorway of the dining room. "Hi," I said and stepped forward to shake hands when I tripped at the edge of the oriental carpet and lurched into him, elbows first. It wasn't a pretty picture. He made a sound like "oomph" because my elbow caught him in the diaphragm. He was too incapacitated for me to fall gracefully into his arms. Instead, I was caught by a drop-dead-beautiful young woman standing at Richard's shoulder.

Crumb, this would be a better story if I'd just lie, but I want truth in romance. And the truth is that the first time I saw Richard Bradshaw after four years of separation, I knocked the wind out of him and was saved from falling on my face by his girlfriend.

THANK YOU VERY MUCH, Rock Hudson and Doris Day

I first learned about sex in the sixth grade from Dawn Grow. Dawn, spelled D-A-W-N, was my best friend, and her brother had given her a book that explained "it" using explicit language and very few euphemisms.

I was appalled that the human race procreated by means of such a grotesque act.

But I was thrilled too. It made all of childhood seem boring. Still, I was positive that my parents, who by then had six or seven children, would not do anything so disgusting. Dawn Grow and I decided quickly that it must be true (her brother's book seemed so authoritative, after all), but it was something a married couple only had to do once, and then an indiscriminate number of children would appear over the next twenty years.

It wasn't until I was thirteen that sex began to make more sense to me. I sat behind the world's most handsome boy in

American History, and I had the strongest urge, a physical urge, to lean forward and kiss the back of his gorgeous neck, which always smelled of Old Spice aftershave.

What was a young girl to do with all this new, hormonal energy?

I received the answer at Mutual at the yearly "Chastity Nights," as my friends and I called them. The answer was that I was to do absolutely nothing until I was married. I was to save "it" for my husband. This was demonstrated with various metaphorical examples: "Would we want to be," the speaker asked, "like a rose that had been passed around the room and examined by curious fingers poking at us, noses sniffling at us, until our petals were limp and discolored, until we were faded before our time? Would we want to present ourselves to our future husbands as toast with all the butter licked off by others?"

For me, in 1956, the answer was a definite no.

So I repeat the question. What was a young woman to do with all this new hormonal energy until she married?

I know what I did. I began to look for a husband at age thirteen. This had its drawbacks, because every attractive boy then became a prospective husband, that is, a prospective sexual partner. The result of this embarrassing dilemma was that I could no longer talk to attractive boys. I became tongue-tied.

I sought help from the only models available to me in 1956: Rock Hudson and Doris Day. You will remember that Rock Hudson and Doris Day were the leading box office draws in the fifties. Their romantic comedies showed us how male-female relationships worked, and I studied them religiously.

I thought the two of them were so witty: "I know I've sown a few wild oats," Rock says to Doris at the end of *Lover Come Back*.

"A few wild oats!" Doris exclaims. "You could apply for a farm loan with the wild oats you've sown."

I loved Rock Hudson, who was handsome as Apollo. He was humorous and a little naughty, but he always ended up committed, if it was the right girl. Doris Day was always the right girl. She was pure and upstanding and pretty — she wore those cute boxy suits with the matching hats designed by "Irene" of Hollywood.

I wanted to be like Doris Day to Rock Hudson: glamorous, witty, rich, and in love. The disparity between my life then and those romantic comedies, which I idolized, was so great that the only choices were suicide or a sense of humor. I chose humor. It was a good choice, because I have since realized that I never was the romantic heroine of my own life. I was never Doris Day. I was Thelma Ritter, her comic maid. I was Eve Arden, Rosalind Russell's quipping friend. I was never Mary Richards, played by Mary Tyler Moore. I was Rhoda Morgenstern. I wasn't even Lucy. I was Ethel. I have always been the sidekick: Sancho Panza, Gabby Hayes, and Jingles, all rolled into one.

To illustrate the disparity of my life and the movies, I will describe the worst date I ever went on. It was a blind date, and it was set up by the sister of my friend Ruth. Three boys needed three dates. Ruth said she would get two of her friends to go along.

I did not want to go. Ruth said it would be fun. I said no, I would not go.

"Please," she said, "it will be fun."

I said, "Don't ask me again. It will be awful."

But Ruth insisted it would be fun. *She* would be there. *Joyce* would be there. What was there to worry about?

I don't know how she got me to go. Maybe she said something like, "You don't have to marry him, for pity's sake!" Maybe she said, "Are you going to be one of those girls who just plays volleyball all of your life?" In any case, I went.

We waited, the three of us, in Ruth's second-story bedroom, which had a window looking out onto the street. I was tremulous with expectation. There was always a chance, albeit slim, that someone *nice* looking with a *nice* personality would show up.

A Chevy with a low-slung back end and an open muffler stopped in front of the house. That did not bode well. Nice boys did not have their mufflers open.

The driver got out first. He was a tall, athletic-looking blond boy wearing a letter jacket from a school across town. He wasn't bad. "He's mine," said Ruth. "I've seen a picture of him."

Then another boy, dark and swarthy, but also not bad, got out. "He's Joyce's," Ruth said with absolute authority.

I waited, holding my breath. Out stepped a short, under-nourished boy, his shoulders hunched into a black vinyl jacket, his hair swept up off his neck in an oily ducktail.

"He's awful!" I cried.

"He's yours," said Ruth.

He was, I learned down in the living room, about five inches shorter than I — a fact that I considered catastrophic. His name was Paul, and he was clueless. I handed him my coat, and I could tell from the blank look on his face that he had not an idea in the world of what to do with it. "Could you help me on with my coat?" I prodded. He looked at me blankly. His friend, the blond athlete, nudged him into action.

The six of us went to the all-state high school basketball tournament. My high school was playing, so everyone I knew in the world was there. Everyone in my high school would see me with this little, greasy dork. What I know now, and didn't know then, is that no one was looking. No one cared who I was with. They were all worrying about themselves. But not knowing this important fact then, I was miserable.

The basketball game was exciting, and we were on our feet most of the time. While we were standing, Ruth elbowed me. Nodding toward Paul, my date, she whispered out of the side of her mouth, "Look, he's standing on his toes."

Sure enough, Paul was standing on his toes, and he remained there for the rest of the night, not just at the basketball game, but later, in downtown Salt Lake, on the way to the Capitol Theater, he still walked on tippy toes. I was mortified. The best part of the date was when he fell asleep during the movie.

Perhaps, somewhere right now, at a *man's* conference — it might be in a bar — Paul is describing the worst date he ever had, a date with a girl the size of a skyscraper.

I saw the humor of the date afterwards. I stayed the night with Ruth, and we laughed about Tall Paul — a name we coined that night and forever. We laughed about a boy who walked on his toes.

I had enough sense of humor to save my own face, but now I wish I could have saved Paul's face as well.

I wish I'd been nicer to you, Paul. I wish I'd asked you questions like those articles on dating in Seventeen *magazine suggested. I wish I'd asked you how many brothers and sisters you had. What was your favorite color, Paul? I never asked you any questions. I never spoke to you at all. I wish I'd poked you in the ribs and made you laugh with a joke:*

— Hey Paul, did you know that they're now replacing laboratory rats with lawyers? There are some things a rat just won't do.

— Knock, knock, Paul.

— Who's there?

— Dwayne.

— Dwayne who?

— Dwayne the bathtub, I'm dwowning.

There was a precedent, Paul, for the way you and I looked together. Sophia Loren married Carlo Ponti, who was a whole head shorter than she was. And speaking of Sophia Loren, do you remember that movie with her and Alan Ladd? He was so much shorter than she, that they dug a trench for her to walk in so that he would appear taller on screen.

We should have dug a trench, Paul, you and I, or I could have walked in the gutter while you walked on the curb with your arm slung loosely around my shoulder. We should have laughed together. I never asked your last name. I wish I knew what it was now. I wish I'd been nicer to you, Paul, wherever you are.

I did not marry anyone remotely resembling Rock Hudson or Tall Paul. I married Tom Plummer. We grew up in the same ward, in the same neighborhood, but he was three years older than I, so we didn't run in the same circles. He went on his mission when I was a junior in high school. I thought about him while he was gone. I was already attracted to him.

He appealed to me for four reasons:
1. He was smart.
2. He was kind to the old ladies in our ward.
3. He played the piano beautifully.
4. He had a perverse sense of humor.

Even now, these seem like pretty good criteria for finding a mate.

He gave his missionary homecoming talk on my twentieth birthday. I wore a red paisley dress with a matching belt — it was a dress that made me feel as beautiful as Doris Day. I sat at the far left side of the chapel next to the window about six rows back. Tom's talk was built around the parable of the sower. It was the best missionary homecoming talk I had ever heard. I was smitten.

But I didn't get his attention until almost a year later. It was after Mutual — we still had M-Men and Gleaners then. I knew Tom was in the building, so I asked Harley Busby if he would accompany me while I sang — I often did that. I sang loud. Maybe I sang "Embraceable You" or "Night and Day" or "You're Just Too Marvelous for Words." I sang and knew that Tom would come. And soon he stood in the doorway of the chapel, and I could see that he saw me for the first time. He saw exactly what I wanted him to see: I was one sexy woman.

That Saturday night we went on our first date. We went to the movies at the Tower Theater, which was then in its artsy period — they served coffee in the lobby. We saw an Ingmar Bergman picture, where a woman confronts a priest who is also her lover and says, "You don't love me anymore, do you? It's my eczema, isn't it?" And she holds out her hands, which are covered with an ugly, lumpy rash.

Tom and I snorted and stifled our laughter.

The next day a sister stood up in testimony meeting and said she was grateful to the Lord for curing her eczema.

From the back of the chapel I looked at Tom, who was sitting at the organ, and we shared a silent guffaw. In that moment I knew we would marry.

To have a sense of humor is to see the disparity between fantasy and reality. It means seeing the pretense, the contradictions, and imperfections in our lives. It is realizing that unlike Doris Day and Sophia Loren, we have no script to give us clever lines and no direction in italics to tell us how to act. We have no dress rehearsals.

To have a sense of humor is also to see our sadness. I was sad that I was never as popular, as smart, as articulate, as beautiful as the girl seated in the next aisle. I am sad now that I let opportunities slip by, that I am no longer young, that I am still flawed, and that I too must die.

Laughter is a reaction to being alive in an imperfect and mortal world, a world where even Rock Hudson was not what we thought he was. I am thankful to all those people who forced me to distinguish between fantasy and reality:

—Thank you, Rock Hudson and Doris Day.

—Thank you, Dawn Grow.

—Thank you, handsome boy in American History.

—Thanks a whole bunch, Ruth.

—Thank you, Tall Paul.

—But especially, thank you, Tom Plummer.